GCSE AQA Combined Science

Biology

Required Practicals

There's no denying it, GCSE Required Practicals can be tricky — your results might not be quite right, you keep running out of time, and your lab partner wouldn't necessarily be your first choice...

That's where this booklet comes in! It has heaps of write-in activities to develop your analysis and evaluation skills for all seven Required Practicals. Plus, it has plenty of exam-style practice — so you'll have everything you need to be an AQA practicals pro.

We've even thrown in example answers for each task, and a mark-by-mark breakdown for every exam-style question — all available in your **free** Online Edition. You can thank us later.

Unlock your Digital Extras

This booklet includes a **free Online Edition** including **full answers**. To access them, just scan the QR code below or go to **cgpbooks.co.uk/extras**, then enter this code!

0730 6950 1561 1201

By the way, this code only works for one person. If somebody else has used this book before you, they might have already claimed the code.

Course Booklet
Higher Level

Published by CGP

From original material by Richard Parsons

Editors: Emily Forsberg, Andy Hurst, Sarah Pattison, Claire Plowman, Camilla Sheridan.

Contributors: Philip Armstrong, Gillian Bridger, Lauren Burns, Paddy Gannon.

With thanks to Beth Linnane for the copyright research.

With thanks to Science Photo Library for the image on page 5 and page 7.

ISBN: 978 1 83774 188 5
Printed by Elanders Ltd, Newcastle upon Tyne.
Illustrations by: Sandy Gardner Artist, email sandy@sandygardner.co.uk
Clipart from Corel®

Text, design, layout and original illustrations © Coordination Group Publications Ltd (CGP) 2024. All rights reserved.

This booklet contains procedures for practical activities. The procedures are covered in outline only and are not intended to be followed in the lab. Safety when carrying out practical work is the responsibility of schools and colleges. A full risk assessment should always be undertaken. CGP cannot be held responsible for any type of loss, damage or injury resulting from the content of these activities.

Photocopying this book is not permitted, even if you have a CLA licence.
Extra copies are available from CGP with next day delivery • 0800 1712 712 • www.cgpbooks.co.uk

Name: Omolola

GCSE AQA Combined Science

Biology

Required Practicals

New!

Course Booklet

Higher Level

CGP

Answers Available Online

CGP

CGP has everything students need for AQA GCSE Science!

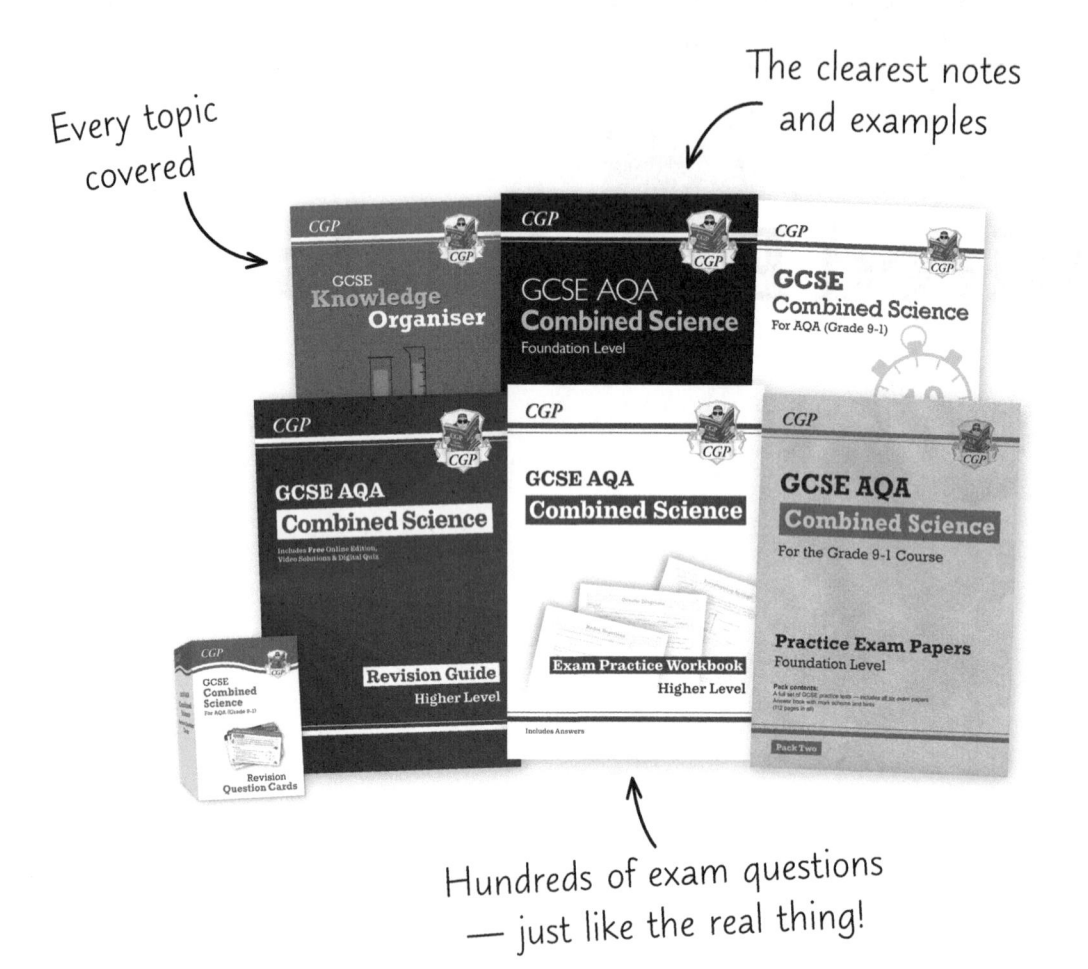

Every topic covered

The clearest notes and examples

Hundreds of exam questions — just like the real thing!

www.cgpbooks.co.uk

Contents

✓ Use the tick boxes to check off the pages you've completed.

Practical 1 — Microscopy

Background Knowledge .... 2 ☐
Practical .... 4 ☐
Results and Analysis .... 6 ☐
Evaluation .... 8 ☐
Exam-Style Questions .... 9 ☐

Practical 2 — Osmosis

Background Knowledge .... 10 ☐
Practical .... 12 ☐
Results and Analysis .... 14 ☐
Conclusions and Evaluation .... 16 ☐
Exam-Style Questions .... 18 ☐

Practical 3 — Food Tests

Background Knowledge .... 19 ☐
Practical .... 20 ☐
Results and Analysis .... 22 ☐
Conclusions and Evaluation .... 23 ☐
Exam-Style Questions .... 24 ☐

Practical 4 — Enzymes

Background Knowledge .... 25 ☐
Practical .... 27 ☐
Results and Analysis .... 29 ☐
Conclusions and Evaluation .... 31 ☐
Exam-Style Questions .... 33 ☐

Practical 5 — Photosynthesis

Background Knowledge .... 34 ☐
Practical .... 36 ☐
Results and Analysis .... 38 ☐
Conclusions and Evaluation .... 40 ☐
Exam-Style Questions .... 42 ☐

Practical 6 — Reaction Time

Background Knowledge .... 43 ☐
Practical .... 45 ☐
Results and Analysis .... 47 ☐
Conclusions and Evaluation .... 48 ☐
Exam-Style Questions .... 49 ☐

Practical 7 — Field Investigations

Background Knowledge .... 50 ☐
Practical — Activity 1 .... 52 ☐
Results and Analysis .... 53 ☐
Practical — Activity 2 .... 54 ☐
Results and Analysis .... 55 ☐
Conclusions and Evaluation .... 56 ☐
Exam-Style Questions .... 58 ☐

Practical 1: Microscopy

Required Practical 1

Background Knowledge

Ever wanted to see what the inside of your cheek looks like really close up? What about an onion? Well you're in luck — this practical's all about **using microscopes** to view **animal** and **plant cells**.

Task 1 Identify which cell below is the **animal cell**, and which is the **plant cell**, then label the **subcellular structures**. Two labels have been added already.

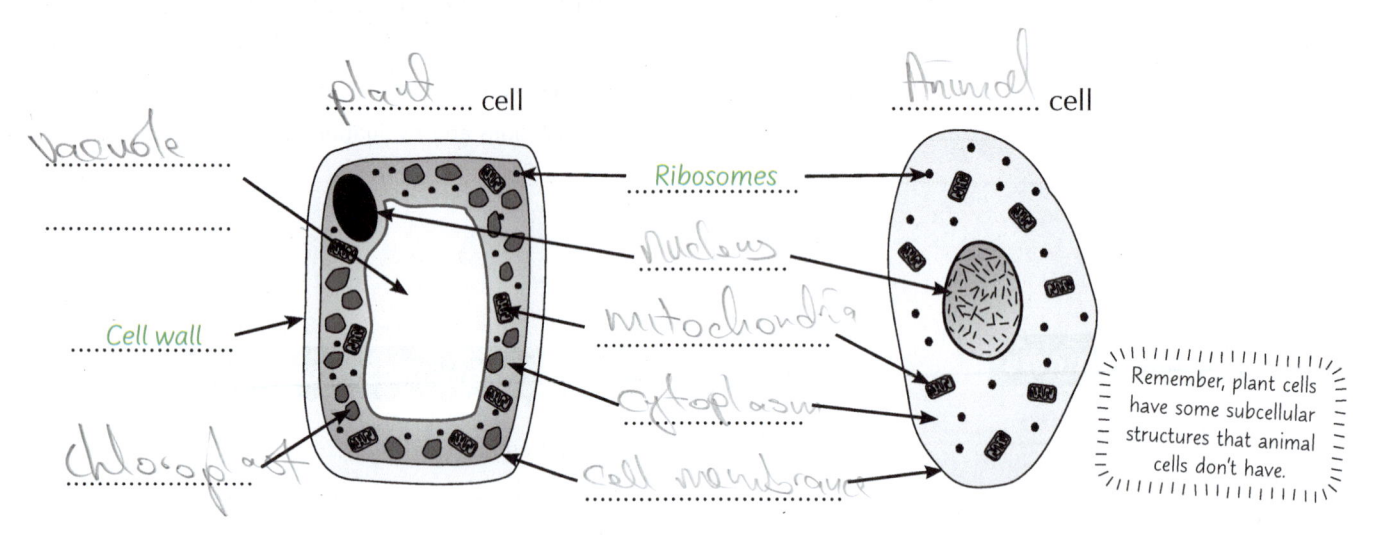

plant cell — Vacuole, Cell wall, Chloroplast, Ribosomes, Nucleus, Mitochondria, Cytoplasm, Cell membrane

Animal cell

Remember, plant cells have some subcellular structures that animal cells don't have.

Task 2 Fill in the **gaps** below using the correct words from the word bank.

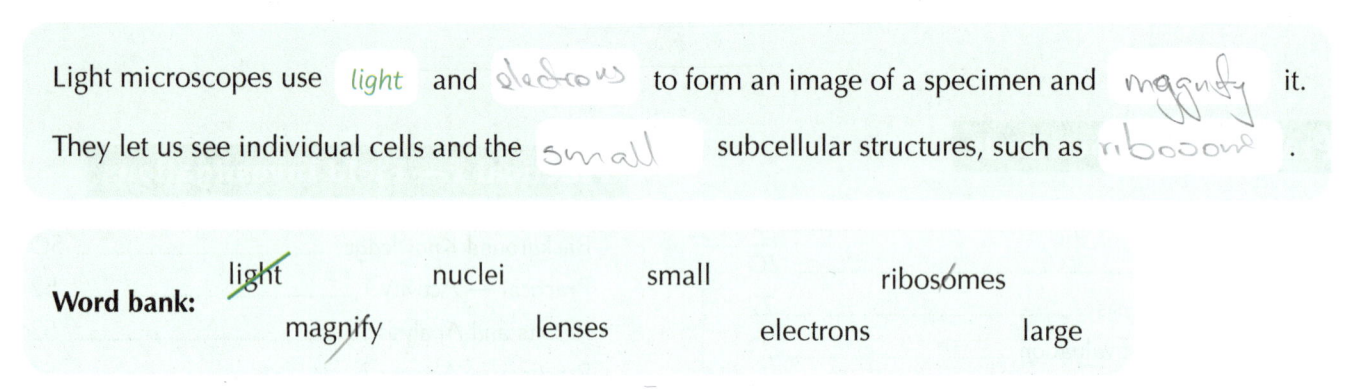

Light microscopes use *light* and *electrons* to form an image of a specimen and *magnify* it. They let us see individual cells and the *small* subcellular structures, such as *ribosomes*.

Word bank: ~~light~~   nuclei   small   ribosomes   magnify   lenses   electrons   large

Task 3 Rearrange the **magnification formula** below to show how to calculate **image size** and **real size**.

Key Definition
Magnification
How much bigger an image is than the real object.

It might help you to use this formula triangle:

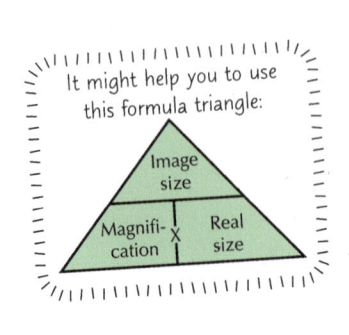

(Formula triangle: Image size on top, Magnification × Real size on bottom)

$$\text{magnification} = \frac{\text{image size}}{\text{real size}}$$

image size =   real size =

Background Knowledge

Required Practical 1

Task 4 Complete the **table** below to show how to **convert** between **units of measurement**.

To convert:

× 1000

× 1000

Unit	How many millimetres it is
Millimetre (mm)	1 mm
Micrometre (µm)	÷ 1000
Nanometre (nm)	÷ 1000

To convert:

÷ 1000

÷ 1000

Task 5 Complete the following **calculations**.

What is the magnification of the microscope if your specimen is 0.06 mm wide and the magnified image is 6 mm wide?

$$\frac{6}{0.06} =$$

× ....

What is the magnification of the microscope if your specimen is 35 µm wide and the magnified image is 52.5 mm wide?

Make sure your units are the same when doing your calculations.

× ....

What is the size of the magnified image if your specimen is 650 nm wide and the magnification of the microscope is × 2000? Give your answer in mm.

.... mm

What is the real size of your specimen if the size of the magnified image is 14 mm wide and the magnification of the microscope is × 400? Give your answer in mm in standard form.

.... mm

Standard form is given as A × 10^n, where A is a number between 1 and 10.
E.g. 1200 is written as 1.2 × 10^3 and 0.00068 is written as 6.8 × 10^{-4}.

Pinch page with two fingers to magnify...

DISCUSS The maximum magnification achievable with a light microscope is usually about × 1500 or × 2000. Why do you think this is? What would happen if you magnified beyond × 2000? Research with a partner.

© CGP — not to be photocopied

Practical 1: Microscopy

Required Practical 1 — Practical

Procedure — Preparing Your Slides

1. For **onion cells**, a drop of **water** is added to a clean slide, then tweezers are used to peel some **tissue** from a single layer of **onion**. This tissue is placed into the water on the slide.
2. For **cheek cells**, a cotton bud is scraped gently along the inside of a person's **cheek**, then rubbed onto a clean microscope slide.
3. The cells are then **stained** — **iodine solution** is used for the onion cells, and **methylene blue** is used for the cheek cells.
4. A **cover slip** is added on top of the **specimens** — excess staining solution can be removed by touching a paper towel to one edge of the cover slip.

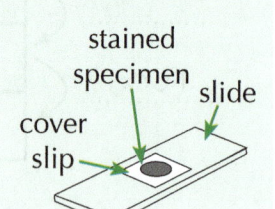

Task 6 Answer the following questions about **staining**.

What apparatus could you use to add one drop of staining solution to a specimen?
A pipette

What is the purpose of staining a specimen?
to make the cell structure visible

Task 7 The table below shows the steps needed to view a specimen with a light microscope, but they're in the wrong order. Write the correct order in the boxes underneath the table, then use the words in **bold** to add the missing labels to the diagram of a light microscope on the right.

1	Use the **coarse adjustment knob** to move the stage to just below the objective lens.
2	Swap to a **higher-powered objective lens** and refocus if you need a greater magnification.
3	Clip the prepared slide onto the **stage**.
4	Select the **lowest-powered objective lens** (the one with the lowest magnification).
5	Adjust the focus with the **fine adjustment knob** until you get a clear image.
6	Look down the **eyepiece** and use the coarse adjustment knob to move the stage down until the image is roughly in focus.

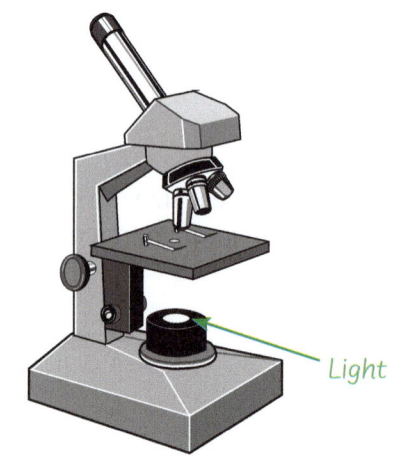

Correct order:

Hint: the lowest-powered objective lens is the shortest, and the highest-powered objective lens is the longest.

Practical 1: Microscopy

Practical

Required Practical 1

Task 8 The images below show cheek cells and onion cells as seen under a light microscope. Produce a **labelled scientific drawing** of some of the cells from each specimen.

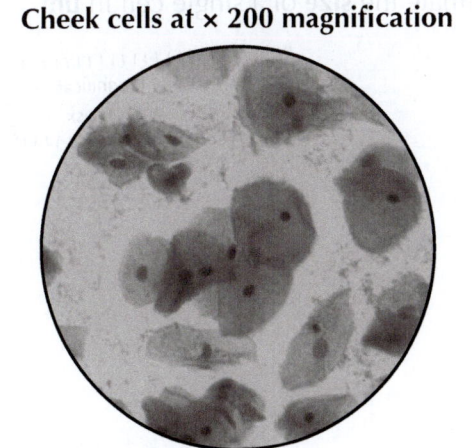

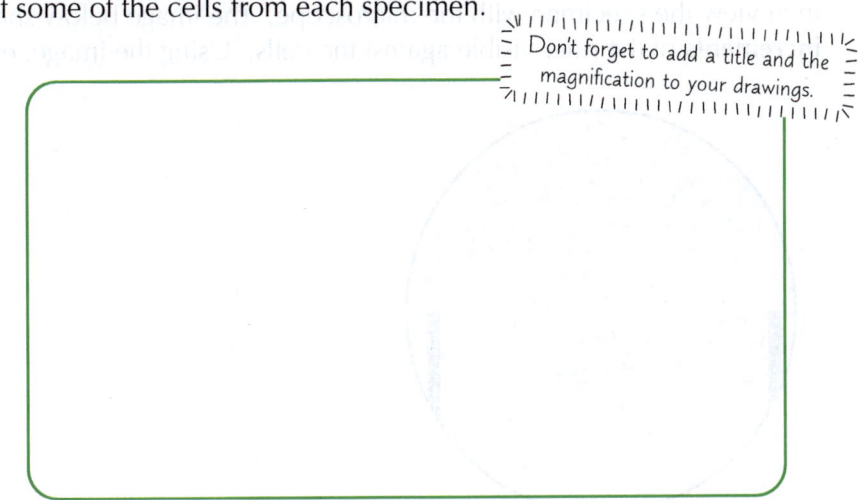

Don't forget to add a title and the magnification to your drawings.

Cheek cells at × 200 magnification

DR GOPAL MURTI / SCIENCE PHOTO LIBRARY

Onion cells at × 100 magnification

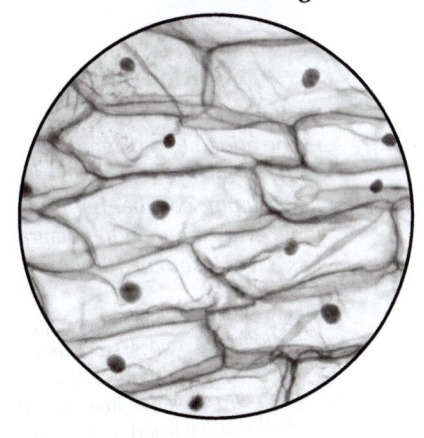

Task 9 The student viewed the onion cells again, this time using a **× 4** objective lens and a **× 10** eyepiece lens. Calculate the **total magnification** used to observe the onion cells.

Hint: the lenses are making the specimen 4× bigger, then 10× bigger.

× ....

Task 10 Why will you not see smaller subcellular structures such as ribosomes in the cells viewed through your light microscope, even if you increased the magnification?

....

....

Key Definition
Resolution
The ability to distinguish between two points (a higher resolution gives a more detailed image).

I'll cell you these drawings for a fiver...

DISCUSS Light is refracted when it moves from glass to air, which can make your specimens hard to see when using magnifications of × 1000 or more. How can this be overcome? Research with a partner.

© CGP — not to be photocopied

Practical 1: Microscopy

Required Practical 1: Results and Analysis

Task 11 To estimate the size of a single cell, you can clip a clear **ruler** on top of a microscope slide, then view the specimen with the microscope. The image below shows an example of this, with the **1 mm increments** of the ruler visible against the cells. Using the image, estimate the **size** of a single cell in **μm**.

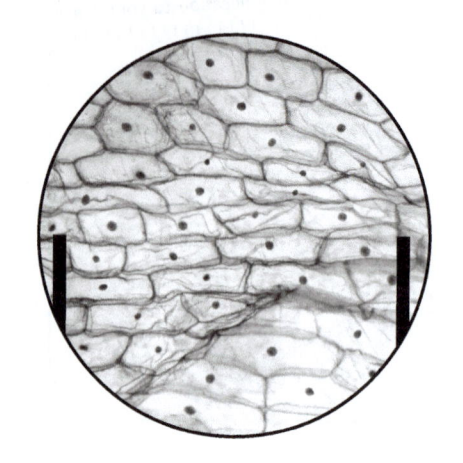

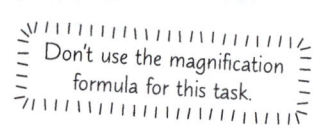

Don't use the magnification formula for this task.

~ .... μm

Task 12 A student has drawn one of the cells from the image above. This is shown below. Use the **formula** below to calculate the **scale bar length** for a **500 μm** scale bar and add it to the student's drawing.

$$\text{scale bar length (μm)} = \frac{\text{drawn length of cell (μm)} \times 500}{\text{actual length of cell (μm)}}$$

Key Definition
Scale bar
A line added to a diagram to show its relative real size. E.g. if a 100 μm scale bar is 1 mm long, every 1 mm in the diagram has a real length of 100 μm.

Measure the student's drawing to find the drawn length of the cell. Use your calculation from Task 11 as the actual length of the cell.

Calculate the length of the scale bar using the formula, and convert this to mm.

.... mm

Add the scale bar to the student's drawing.

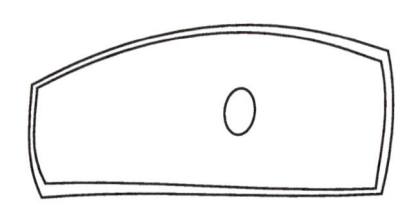

Practical 1: Microscopy

Results and Analysis

Required Practical 1

Task 13 What feature of the cells in Task 11 tells you they are **plant cells**?

....

Task 14 Another student has drawn the cells below. Use them to make the following **estimations**.

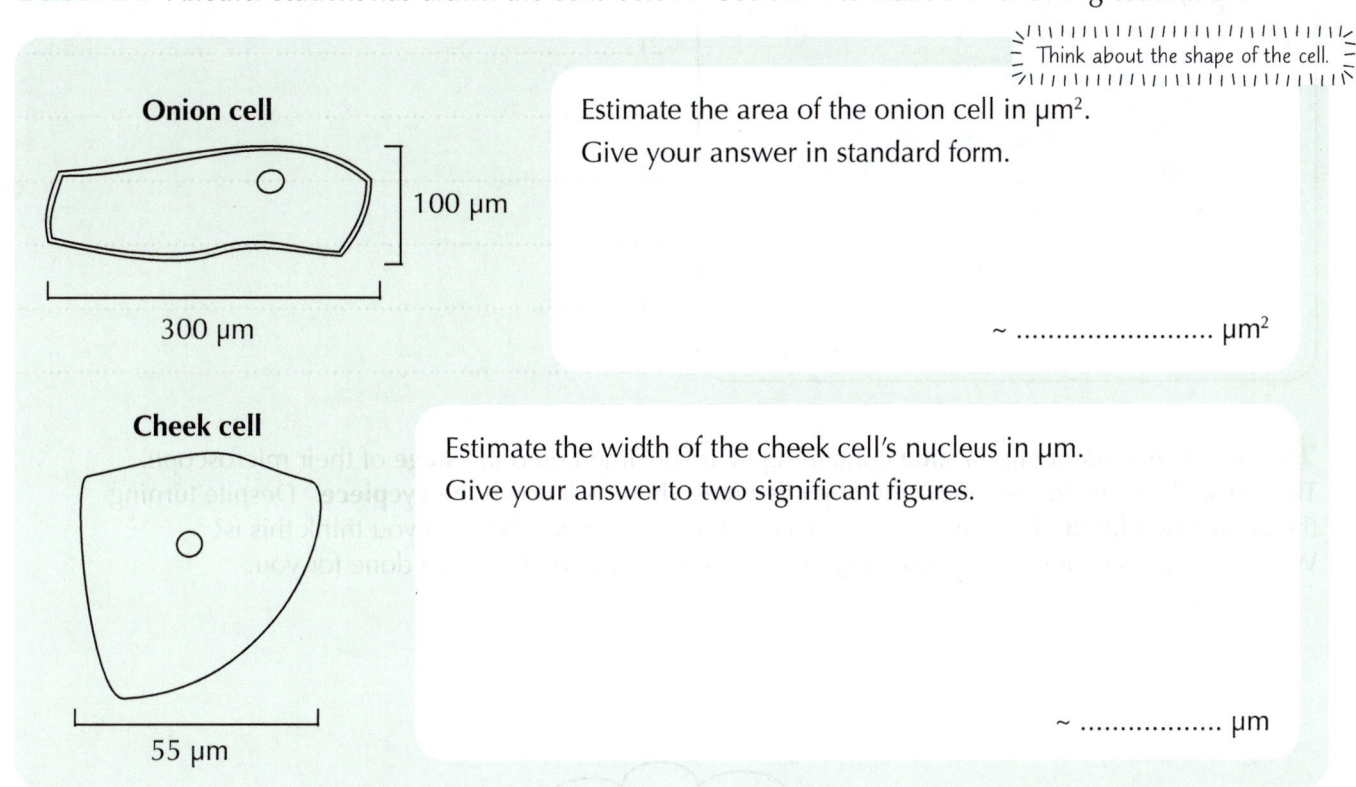

Think about the shape of the cell.

Onion cell

100 μm
300 μm

Estimate the area of the onion cell in μm². Give your answer in standard form.

~ .... μm²

Cheek cell

55 μm

Estimate the width of the cheek cell's nucleus in μm. Give your answer to two significant figures.

~ .... μm

Task 15 The magnification that the cells were viewed at was increased. Use the **magnification formula** to answer the following questions.

Flick back to p.2 if you've forgotten the magnification formula.

The image below shows a cheek cell at × 600 magnification. What is its real width?

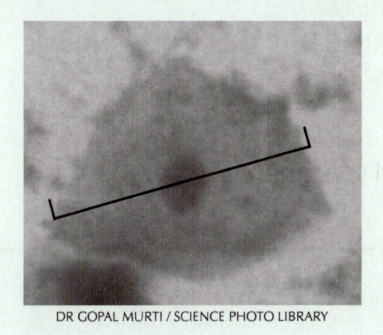

DR GOPAL MURTI / SCIENCE PHOTO LIBRARY

.... μm

The image below shows an onion cell with a real width of 320 μm. What magnification has been used?

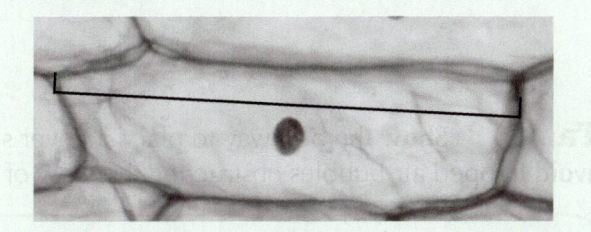

× ....

© CGP — not to be photocopied

Practical 1: Microscopy

Required Practical 1: Evaluation

Task 16 A student has drawn the **diagram** below of some onion cells as seen through a light microscope. Identify **four flaws** in the student's drawing.

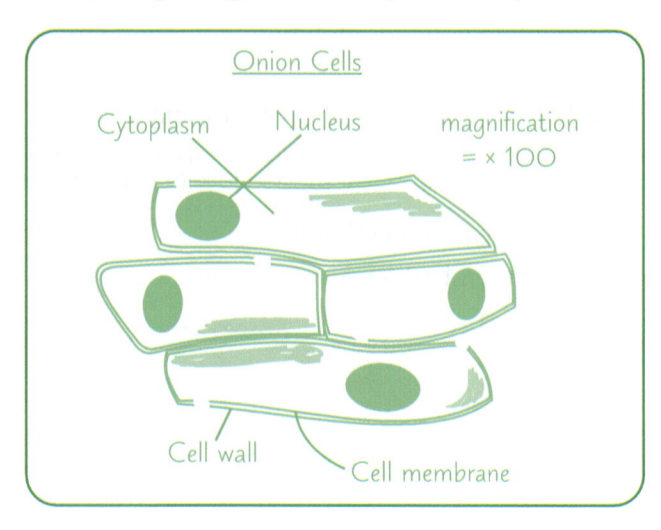

Onion Cells
- Cytoplasm
- Nucleus
- magnification = × 100
- Cell wall
- Cell membrane

1) ....
....
2) ....
....
3) ....
....
4) ....
....

Task 17 A student clips a **slide** containing their specimen onto the **stage** of their microscope. They raise the stage to just below the **objective lens**, then look down the **eyepiece**. Despite turning the **adjustment knob**, they can't see an image of their specimen. Why do you think this is? Write your suggestions in the **mind map** below. One suggestion has been done for you.

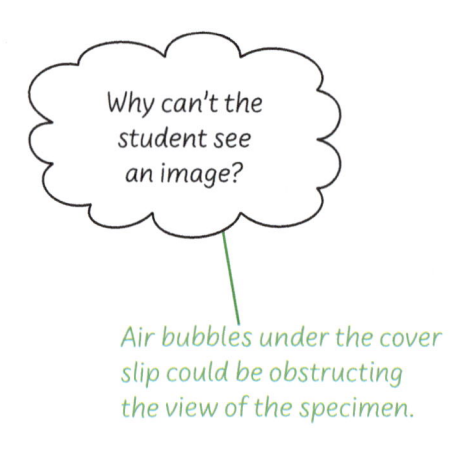

Why can't the student see an image?

Air bubbles under the cover slip could be obstructing the view of the specimen.

Task 18 **Show** the best way to place a cover slip over a stained specimen in order to **avoid** trapped air bubbles obstructing the view of the specimen.

DISCUSS — **Use a × 2000 lens to measure your willpower to go on...**
Are there any other ways you can think of to estimate the size of cells and their subcellular structures? Can you think of any other golden rules for good scientific drawings? Share ideas with your partner.

Practical 1: Microscopy

Exam-Style Questions

Required Practical 1

Task 19 Try these **exam-style** questions.

1 A student is investigating the size and structure of plant cells. They add a thin slice of onion tissue to a drop of water on a clean microscope slide, and stain it with iodine solution. They then add a cover slip on top of their specimen and clip their slide onto the stage of a light microscope.

1.1 Suggest why the specimen needs to be thin.

....
....
[1]

1.2 The student views their specimen with the lowest-powered objective lens. They then want to increase the total magnification to × 400 and refocus on their specimen. Describe how they should do this using the parts of the microscope labelled in **Figure 1**.

Figure 1

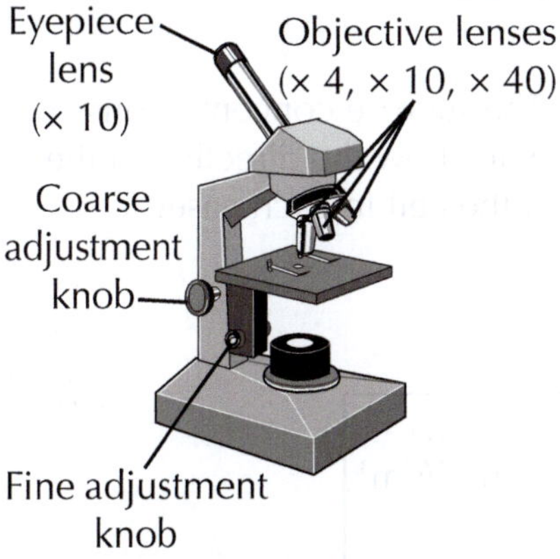

Eyepiece lens (× 10)
Objective lenses (× 4, × 10, × 40)
Coarse adjustment knob
Fine adjustment knob

....
....
....
....
....
....
....
[4]

1.3 The student views their specimen with the light microscope. **Figure 2** shows an onion cell at × 100 magnification. Calculate the real width of the onion cell using the magnification formula.

Figure 2

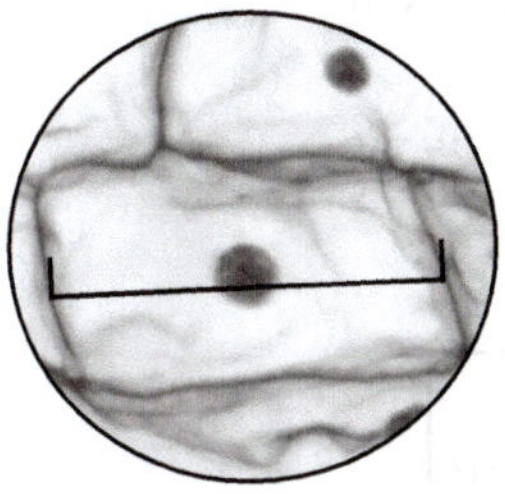

real width = ... μm
[4]

1.4 The student's teacher suggests that when determining the size of a particular type of cell, at least three cells should be measured and a mean average size should be calculated. Explain why the teacher has made this suggestion.

....
[1]

[Total 10 marks]

© CGP — not to be photocopied

Practical 1: Microscopy

Practical 2: Osmosis

Background Knowledge

This practical is about **osmosis**. You will investigate the effect that **different concentrations** of **sugar** solution have on **plant cells**, using pieces of potato. And at the end, you'll have prepared a sugary snack — nice*.

Task 1 Fill in the blanks to complete the definition of **osmosis**:

Osmosis is the movement of water molecules across a partially permeable membrane from a region of .... water concentration to a region of .... water concentration.

Task 2 Circle the solution below that has the highest **water** concentration.

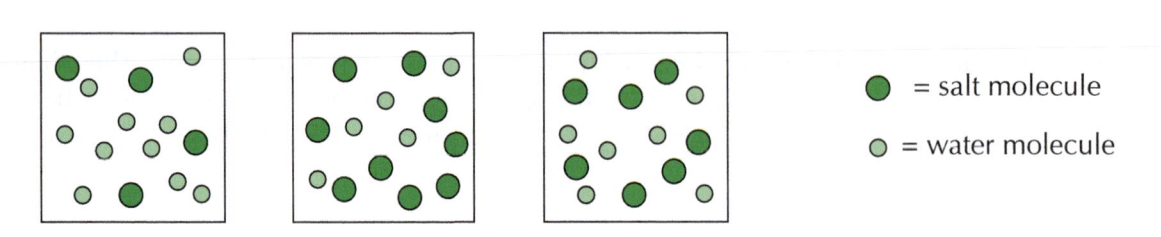

● = salt molecule
○ = water molecule

Task 3 Each diagram below shows a cell in a sucrose solution. The sucrose concentrations inside and outside the cells are shown. For each cell, draw an arrow to show the direction of the net movement of **water** molecules. What will happen to the **mass** of the cell in each case? The first one has been done for you.

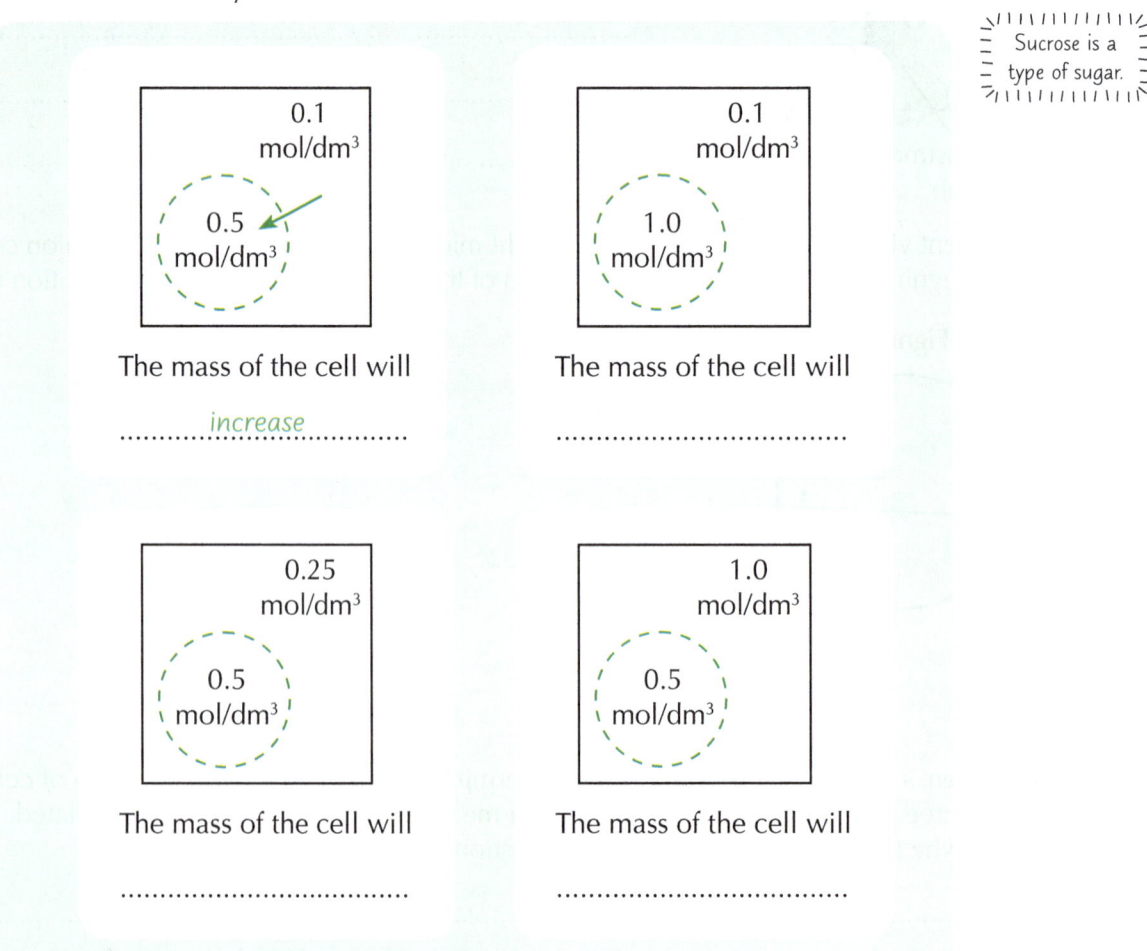

Sucrose is a type of sugar.

Outside: 0.1 mol/dm³, Inside: 0.5 mol/dm³
The mass of the cell will *increase*

Outside: 0.1 mol/dm³, Inside: 1.0 mol/dm³
The mass of the cell will ....

Outside: 0.25 mol/dm³, Inside: 0.5 mol/dm³
The mass of the cell will ....

Outside: 1.0 mol/dm³, Inside: 0.5 mol/dm³
The mass of the cell will ....

*Disclaimer — no practical results (or apparatus) should ever be consumed under any circumstance. Try a regular biscuit when you're done instead.

Background Knowledge

Required Practical 2

Task 4 A cell is shown on the right. It's put into a salt solution. Draw lines to connect the **type of solution** it's put into to what the cell will **look like** after spending some time in the solution.

A salt solution that is...　　　　　　　　　Cell will look like:

...more dilute than the contents of the cell.

...more concentrated than the contents of the cell.

...the same concentration as the contents of the cell.

Task 5 Water is being taken up into a root cell by osmosis. What does that tell you about the **concentration of water** inside the root cell compared to the concentration in the surrounding soil?

....

Which of these things would you expect to **speed up** the rate of osmosis?

- A higher temperature ☐
- More minerals in the soil ☐
- More water in the soil ☐
- A smaller root cell ☐

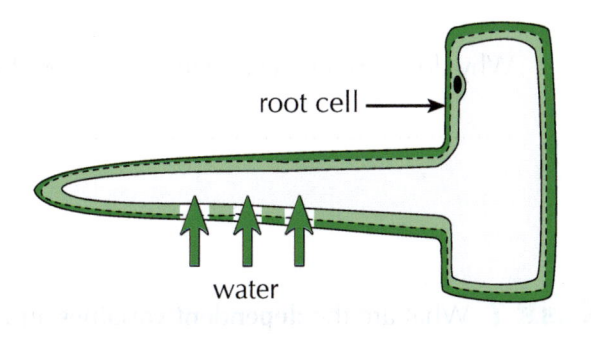

For a topic all about water, osmosis is pretty dry...

DISCUSS If you put a gummy bear into a glass of water, the bear swells up and gets bigger due to osmosis. With your partner, come up with an experiment you could do to work out what the sugar concentration is in a gummy bear, using glasses of water, a packet of gummy bears and teaspoons of sugar.

© CGP — not to be photocopied　　　　　　　Practical 2: Osmosis

Required Practical 2 — Practical

Task 6 Read the procedure then answer the following questions.

Procedure

1. Use a cork borer to cut out cylinders from a potato.
2. Use a sharp knife to remove any skin from the cylinders and trim them all to the same length.
3. Measure the mass of each cylinder using a balance with a resolution of 0.01 g.
4. Measure the length of each cylinder.
5. Set up boiling tubes with a range of sugar solutions, plus one tube with just water.
6. Place one cylinder in each boiling tube and leave them for 30 minutes.
7. Take the cylinders out of the solutions and dry them using paper towels.
8. Measure the mass and length of each cylinder again.

A cork borer is a metal tool used for cutting holes or tubes.

Key Definition
Resolution
The smallest change the equipment can detect.

Why is a **cork borer** used to cut the potato, rather than just a knife?

....

....

Why is the **skin removed** from the potato cylinders?

....

Why is the **resolution** of the mass balance important?

....

Why do the potato cylinders need to be **dried** after being removed from the solution?

....

Task 7 What are the **dependent variables** and the **independent variable** for this experiment?

Dependent variables...
....

Independent variable...

Key Definitions
Independent variable
The variable in an experiment that is changed.
Dependent variable
The variable in an experiment that is measured.

Practical 2: Osmosis © CGP — not to be photocopied

Practical

Required Practical 2

Task 8 Fill in the mind map to show variables that need to be **controlled** for this experiment. For the two variables already on the mind map, give a reason why they need to be controlled.

Temperature of the solution   *Type of potato*

Variables to control when investigating the effect of sugar solutions on the mass of potato cylinders.

Key Definition
Control variable
A variable in an experiment that is kept the same.

Variable: *Temperature of the solution*

Reason: ....
....

Variable: *Type of potato*

Reason: ....
....

Task 9 The series of sugar solutions with **different concentrations** are set up by transferring different amounts of 1.0 mol/dm³ sugar solution to a beaker and diluting it with distilled water.

A lab technician wants to make a **0.2 mol/dm³** sugar solution.

10 cm³ of 1.0 mol/dm³ sugar solution has been added to the beaker on the right.

Draw a line on the beaker to show where it should be filled to with distilled water to make a 0.2 mol/dm³ solution.

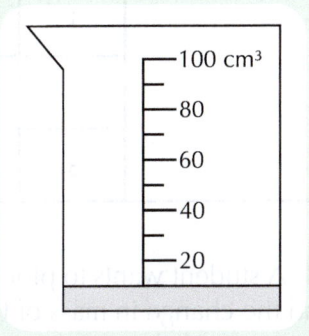

I know a joke about potatoes, but it's not very apeeling...

DISCUSS With a partner, discuss the aim of the experiment outlined in Task 6 — what is it testing, and what would you expect the results to show? Are there any parts of the method that might be tricky to do in order to make it a fair test? And are there any safety precautions that someone following the method should take?

© CGP — not to be photocopied

Practical 2: Osmosis

Results and Analysis

Required Practical 2

Task 10 The diagram below shows the length of a potato cylinder before and after the cylinder was placed in a sugar solution. What is the **change** in length in millimetres?

before [ ]

after [ ]

....

Task 11 The table below shows some example results from an osmosis experiment that used four different concentrations of sugar solution. The experiment was repeated three times. Calculate the **mean** change in mass and length for each concentration.
Then circle the concentrations of the solutions in which the potato samples **lost** water.

Concentration of sugar solution (mol/dm³)	Sample number	Change in mass (g)	Mean change in mass (g)	Change in length (mm)	Mean change in length (mm)
0.0	1	+0.23		+2.0	
0.0	2	+0.20		+1.0	
0.0	3	+0.19		+2.5	
0.25	1	+0.15		+0.5	
0.25	2	+0.17		0.0	
0.25	3	+0.14		+0.5	
0.5	1	-0.22		-0.5	
0.5	2	-0.29		-0.5	
0.5	3	-0.27		-1.0	
1.0	1	-0.48		-1.5	
1.0	2	-0.50		-2.0	
1.0	3	-0.48		-2.0	

Task 12 A student wants to plot a graph to show the relationship between the concentration of the solution and the change in mass of the potato. They calculate the **percentage change** in mass to do this.

Why does the student want to look at percentage change rather than just the change in mass?

....

....

Practical 2: Osmosis

© CGP — not to be photocopied

Results and Analysis

Required Practical 2

Task 13 Complete the table by calculating the **difference in mass** and the **percentage change** in mass for each concentration. Give the percentage change values to the nearest whole number.

Concentration of sugar solution (mol/dm³)	Mass at start (g)	Mass at end (g)	Difference in mass (g)	Percentage change in mass (%)
0.0	2.67	3.15		
0.2	2.73	2.90		
0.4	2.45	2.40		
0.6	2.39	2.20		
0.8	2.84	2.50		
1.0	2.77	2.35		

Task 14 Using the results in the table above, plot a graph of the percentage change in mass against the concentration of sugar solution. Include a **line of best fit**.

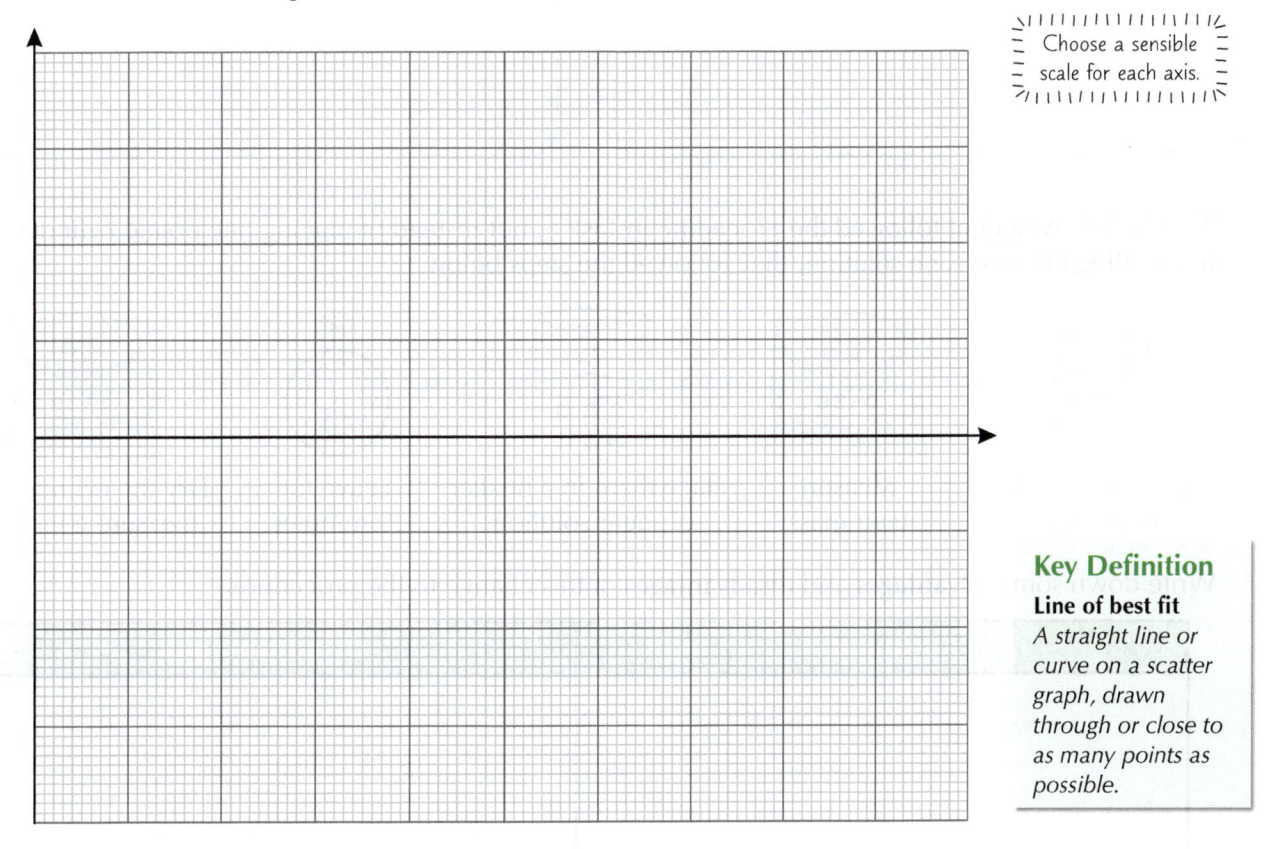

Choose a sensible scale for each axis.

Key Definition
Line of best fit
A straight line or curve on a scatter graph, drawn through or close to as many points as possible.

I really fancy some chips now...

DISCUSS With a partner, discuss what changes you could make to the method for this experiment that would change the shape of a graph of the results like the one above. What changes would give a different intercept (the point at which it crosses the x-axis)? Look back at your mind map in Task 8 for ideas.

© CGP — not to be photocopied

Practical 2: Osmosis

Required Practical 2

Conclusions and Evaluation

Task 15 Using the graph you plotted for Task 14, work out the **concentration** of sugar solution that is **equal** to the concentration of the solution **inside** the potato cell.

The concentration is ☐ mol/dm³.

Explain how you got your answer.

Task 16 For each of the **errors** below, describe how it would affect the results. Could you compensate for the error after it has occurred if you knew about it?

The mass balance isn't calibrated correctly, so it reads 1 g when there's nothing on it.	The pieces of potato are dried using a paper towel. Some are left sitting on the paper before they are weighed.

Task 17 A student followed the procedure in Task 6, but instead of placing one potato cylinder in a boiling tube for each solution, they followed the steps below.

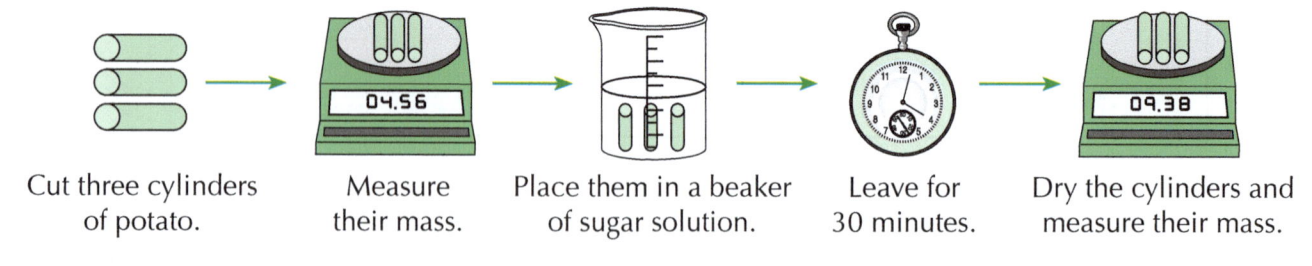

Cut three cylinders of potato. → Measure their mass. → Place them in a beaker of sugar solution. → Leave for 30 minutes. → Dry the cylinders and measure their mass.

Write down some **advantages** and **disadvantages** of this change to the procedure.

Advantages	Disadvantages

Practical 2: Osmosis

Conclusions and Evaluation

Required Practical 2

Task 18 A student says that carrots taste sweeter than potatoes, so they must contain more sugar. The student decides to carry out an experiment to investigate this.

What is the student's **hypothesis**?

....

Key Definition
Hypothesis
A possible explanation for a scientific observation.

The student has a carrot, a potato, a scalpel, a mass balance, a bottle of distilled water and some boiling tubes. How can they use this equipment to **test their hypothesis**?

....
....
....

What **results** would the student expect to see for this experiment? Why?

....
....
....

Explain whether the student could conclude that the **hypothesis is correct** from those results.

....
....
....

Task 19 A rate of change can be calculated by dividing the amount of change by the time taken for the change to occur.

Think about what variables you'd need to measure, change or keep the same.

Write a method for investigating the effect of **temperature** on the **rate of osmosis** for potato cells. Include a list of the apparatus you will need for the investigation.

Method	Apparatus

© CGP — not to be photocopied

Practical 2: Osmosis

Required Practical 2 — **Exam-Style Questions**

Task 20 Try these **exam-style** questions.

1   Some students carried out an experiment to investigate osmosis using Visking tubing. Visking tubing is a partially permeable membrane, so can be used to simulate a cell membrane.
The students filled a length of Visking tubing with sucrose solution A, and placed it into a beaker containing sucrose solution B.
The set up is shown in **Figure 1**.

Figure 1 — sucrose solution B, Visking tubing containing sucrose solution A

The students recorded the mass of the filled tubing at the start of the experiment and then every half an hour, for a total of 4 hours.
Figure 2 shows their results.

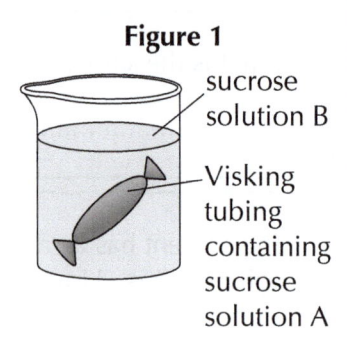

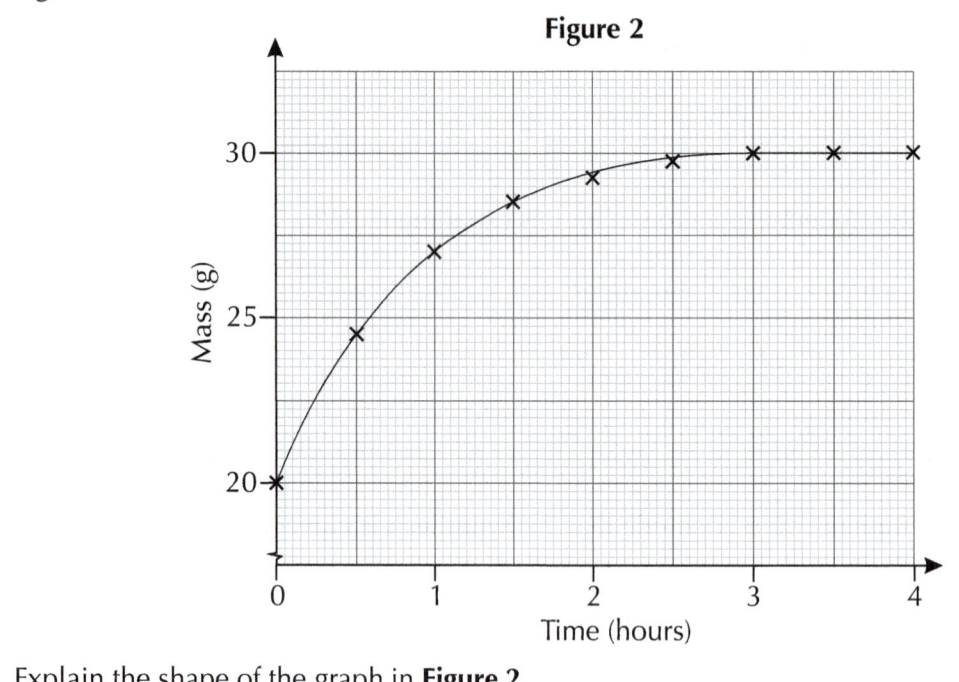

Figure 2 (graph of Mass (g) vs Time (hours), rising from 20 g at 0 hours, through ~24.5 g at 0.5 h, ~27 g at 1 h, ~28.5 g at 1.5 h, ~29.5 g at 2 h, levelling off at 30 g from 2.5 h onwards to 4 h)

1.1 Explain the shape of the graph in **Figure 2**.

....

....

....
[2]

1.2 Calculate the rate of osmosis in the first 30 minutes of the experiment.

.... g/hour
[2]

1.3 Suggest what can be concluded about the concentration of sucrose solution A in relation to the concentration of sucrose solution B at the beginning of the experiment.

....
[1]
[Total 5 marks]

Practical 2: Osmosis

Practical 3: Food Tests

Background Knowledge

Required Practical 3

Your digestive system breaks down **big molecules** from food into **smaller ones**. There are different methods you can use to **identify** whether your food contains **sugars**, **starch**, **lipids** and **proteins**. I hope you're hungry.

Task 1 Fill in the **gaps** in the diagrams below to show what the larger food molecules are **broken down** into.

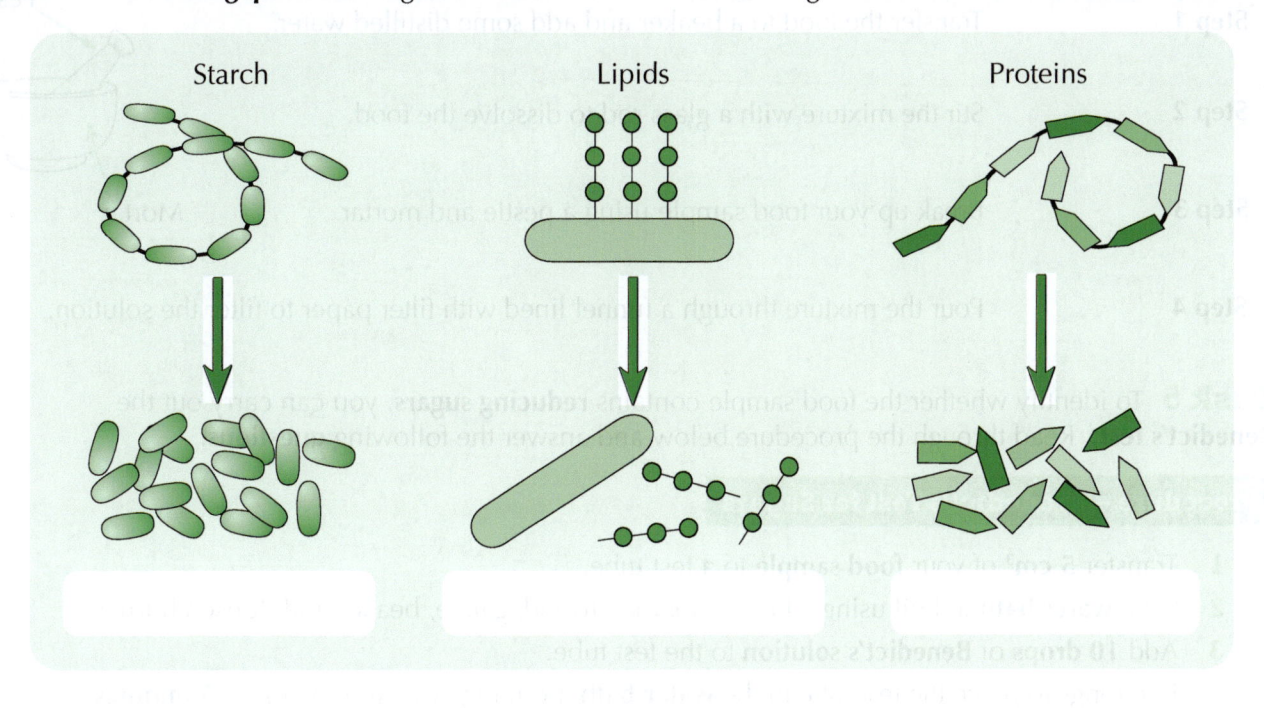

Starch

Lipids

Proteins

Task 2 Answer the following questions about **digestion**.

Why does the body break down bigger food molecules into smaller ones during digestion?
....
....

What does the body use the products of digestion for?
....

Task 3 This practical uses a **Bunsen burner**.
Give **five safety precautions** you should take when using a Bunsen burner.

1) ....

2) ....

3) ....

4) ....

5) ....

© CGP — not to be photocopied

Practical 3: Food Tests

Practical

Required Practical 3

Task 4 In this practical, you need to identify what types of food molecule a **mystery food sample** contains. The steps below show how to **prepare** the food sample for **testing**, but they aren't in order. **Draw lines** to match each **step number** with the **correct description**.

Step 1 — Transfer the food to a beaker and add some distilled water.

Step 2 — Stir the mixture with a glass rod to dissolve the food.

Step 3 — Break up your food sample using a pestle and mortar.

Step 4 — Pour the mixture through a funnel lined with filter paper to filter the solution.

(Pestle, Mortar labelled on diagram)

Task 5 To identify whether the food sample contains **reducing sugars**, you can carry out the **Benedict's test**. Read through the procedure below and answer the following **questions**.

Procedure — Benedict's Test for Sugars

1. Transfer **5 cm³** of your **food sample** to a test tube.
2. Set a **water bath** to boil using a heat proof mat, tripod, gauze, beaker and Bunsen burner.
3. Add **10 drops** of **Benedict's solution** to the test tube.
4. Use tongs to place the test tube in the **water bath** (pointing away from you) for **5 minutes**.
5. Transfer the test tube to a test tube rack with the tongs and **observe the colour** of the solution.

How would you set up a water bath using the equipment in step 2 of the procedure above? Draw a labelled diagram in the box.

What piece of equipment should you use to transfer Benedict's solution to the test tube?

Why does the solution in the test tubes need to be heated?

What equipment should you use to ensure the water bath is at the correct temperature?

DISCUSS — **Who even is Benedict anyway? That guy from Sherlock?**
Discuss with a partner what equipment you should use to measure 5 cm³ of your food sample. How would the size of the graduations of measurement on this equipment affect the uncertainty of your results?

Practical 3: Food Tests

Practical

Required Practical 3

Task 6 The **biuret test** can be used to test whether the food sample contains **proteins**. Use the **diagram** to complete the steps in the procedure below.

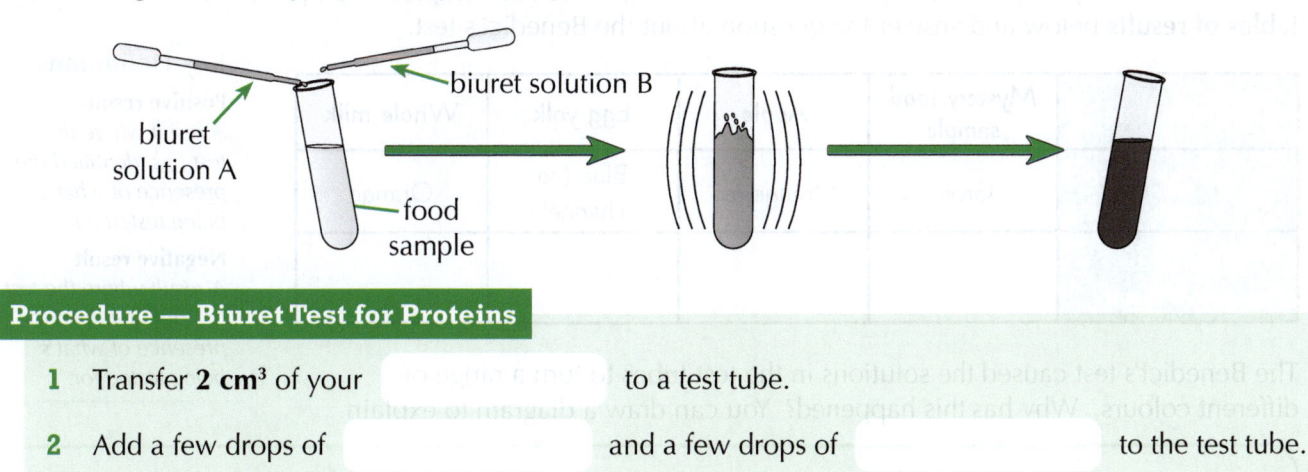

Procedure — Biuret Test for Proteins

1. Transfer **2 cm³** of your _____ to a test tube.
2. Add a few drops of _____ and a few drops of _____ to the test tube.
3. **Mix** the contents by _____ the test tube.
4. **Observe** any _____ within the test tube.

Task 7 Read the procedure for carrying out the **Iodine test** for **starch** and answer the question below.

Procedure — Iodine Test for Starch

1. Transfer **5 cm³** of your **food sample** to a test tube.
2. Add a few drops of **iodine solution** and **mix** by gently shaking the test tube.
3. Observe any **colour change** within the test tube.

Key Definition
Irritant
A substance that can cause inflammation upon contact with the body.

Iodine is an irritant and can stain skin. What safety precautions should you take when handling iodine solution?

....

Task 8 You can carry out the **emulsion test** to check whether a food sample contains **lipids**. Read the procedure below, then answer the question.

Alternative methods can be used to test for lipids, e.g. using Sudan III stain solution.

Procedure — Emulsion Test for Lipids

1. **Prepare** your food sample by breaking it up with a pestle and mortar, then transfer it to a test tube and add **ethanol**.
2. **Shake** the test tube well and leave it to **stand** for a few minutes.
3. Pour the solution into a different test tube containing **distilled water**.
4. Observe whether any **emulsions** form.

Lipids dissolve in ethanol.

Key Definition
Emulsion
A mixture of two liquids that normally don't mix. One liquid forms tiny droplets that are suspended in the other one. The droplets scatter light, causing the liquid to look cloudy.

Ethanol usually mixes with water. Explain why an emulsion indicates that lipids are present.

Practical 3: Food Tests

Results and Analysis

Required Practical 3

Task 9 The food tests in this practical can give **positive** or **negative** results. A class carried out these tests on a **mystery food sample** as well as a few **known food samples**. Complete the **tables of results** below and answer the question about the Benedict's test.

Food sample	Mystery food sample	Apple	Egg yolk	Whole milk
Colour observed after Benedict's test	Green	Orange-red	Blue (no change)	Orange
Positive or negative result?				

Key Definitions

Positive result
A result where the test has identified the presence of what's being tested for.

Negative result
A result where the test has not identified the presence of what's being tested for.

The Benedict's test caused the solutions in the test tubes to turn a range of different colours. Why has this happened? You can draw a diagram to explain.

Food sample	Mystery food sample	Apple	Egg yolk	Whole milk
Colour observed after biuret test				
Positive or negative result?	Positive	Negative	Positive	Positive

If the result is negative, the test solution will remain the original colour.

Food sample	Mystery food sample	Apple	Egg yolk	Whole milk
Colour observed after iodine test	Blue-black	Dark blue	Browny-orange (no change)	Browny-orange (no change)
Positive or negative result?				

Food sample	Mystery food sample	Apple	Egg yolk	Whole milk
Cloudy layer formed after emulsion test?	Yes	No		
Positive or negative result?			Positive	Positive

DISCUSS

Blue-black, cloudy, precipitation — positive for storm...

A positive Benedict's test result forms a precipitate (an insoluble substance). How could you quantify the amount of reducing sugar in a food sample? Discuss with a partner — there's more than one way.*

*Hint: use the Benedict's test on solutions of known concentrations of reducing sugar first.

Practical 3: Food Tests

Conclusions and Evaluation

Required Practical 3

Task 10 Using the **tables of results** on the previous page, what can you **conclude** about the food **molecules** present in each food **sample**? Tick the **correct boxes** below.

	Contains reducing sugar?	Contains proteins?	Contains starch?	Contains lipids?
Mystery food sample	☐	☐	☐	☐
Apple	☐	☐	☐	☐
Egg yolk	☐	☐	☐	☐
Whole milk	☐	☐	☐	☐

Task 11 Two students have made the conclusions below after looking at the results on the previous page. Evaluate the **validity** of their conclusions.

Key Definition
Valid conclusion
A conclusion that is supported by the results of a fair test.

The mystery food sample has a low concentration of reducing sugars.

Is this valid?
☐ Yes
☐ No

Explain why.

The mystery food sample has a high concentration of protein.

Is this valid?
☐ Yes
☐ No

Explain why.

Task 12 Another student criticised the results from this investigation as being **subjective**. Answer the question below about **subjectivity**. Think about how you could overcome this **problem**.

Why might the results from food tests be considered subjective?

....

Key Definition
Subjective
Based on someone's perspective or opinion rather than fact.

Add ways of overcoming this problem to the mind map below.

Ways to avoid subjectivity in food tests.

© CGP — not to be photocopied

Practical 3: Food Tests

Required Practical 3 — Exam-Style Questions

Task 13 Try these **exam-style** questions.

1 A student tested a food sample to see if it contained starch. The procedure they used, and the resulting colour change, are shown in the diagram below.

1.1 Identify solution **A**.

....
[1]

1.2 Suggest what their food sample could have been.

....
[1]

1.3 The student then carried out three repeats of the Benedict's test on another food sample. They used an electric water bath instead of heating a beaker of water with a Bunsen burner. Other than safety benefits, give one advantage of using an electric water bath.

....

....
[1]

1.4 The student's prepared food sample had an orange colour before the test began. Suggest how this could cause an error in the results if the sample contains no reducing sugars.

....

....
[1]

2 A student prepares a food sample by dissolving it in distilled water and filtering it into a beaker.

2.1 Describe a method the student could use to test if the food sample contains proteins. You should include the names of any solutions used.

....

....

....
[3]

2.2 After carrying out the test, the student concludes that their food sample does not contain any proteins. Describe the result you would expect to see from the test. Explain your answer.

....

....
[2]

[Total 9 marks]

Practical 4: Enzymes

Background Knowledge

Required Practical 4

For this practical, you'll be investigating how varying the **pH** affects the rate of **enzyme activity**. Oooh...

Task 1 Complete the diagrams to show the **breakdown** of large molecules into smaller molecules by certain enzymes. The missing words are in the box on the right.

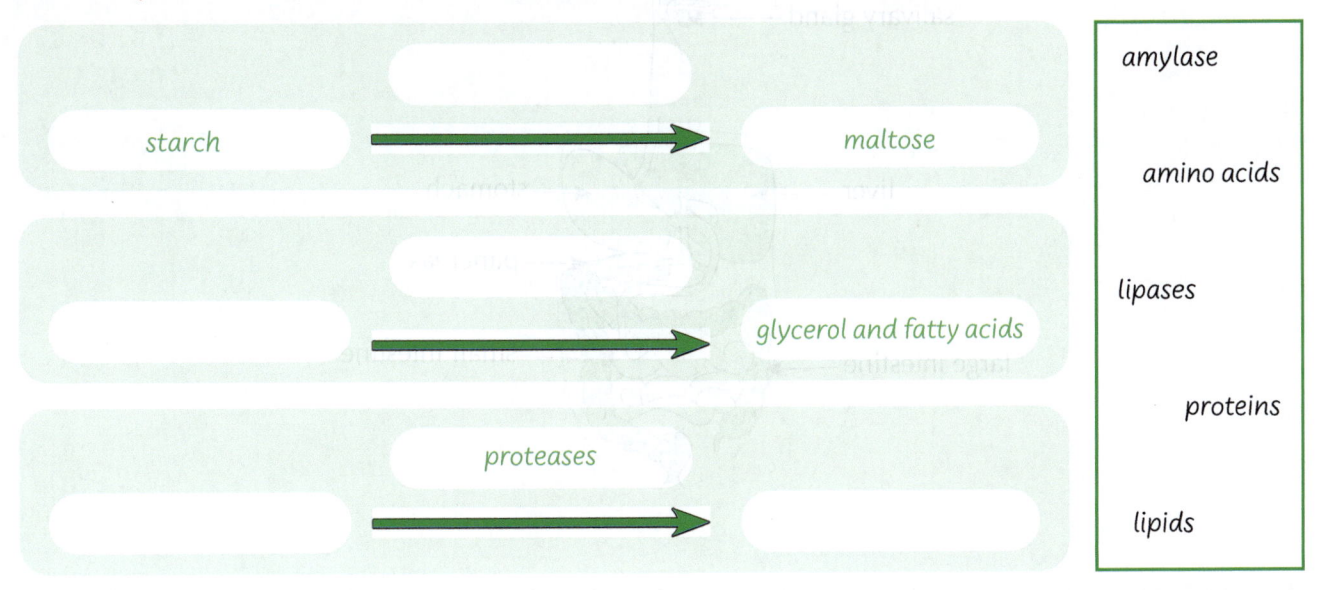

starch → maltose

____ → glycerol and fatty acids

proteases

Word box: amylase, amino acids, lipases, proteins, lipids

Task 2 Iodine solution is used to test for the presence of starch. **Circle** the correct answers below.

What colour is iodine solution?   blue-black   clear   browny-orange   blue-green

What colour does it turn in the presence of starch?   blue-black   clear   browny-orange

Task 3 Complete the sentences about enzymes.
Then draw **lines** to match the enzyme to the substance it binds to.

Enzymes act as biological .... to .... the rate of reactions in metabolism.

Each enzyme has an .... that is specific to the substance it binds to.

This substance is called the ....

Enzyme   **Substance**

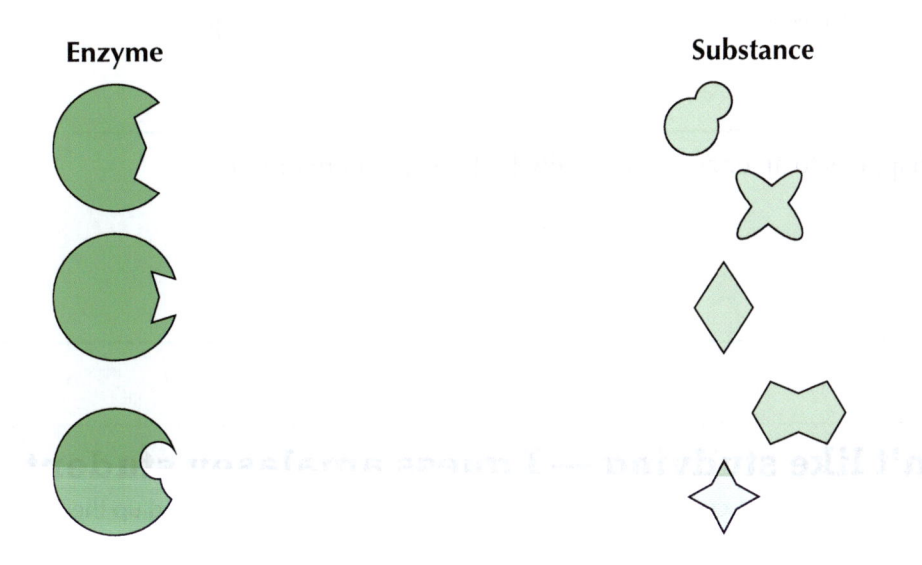

© CGP — not to be photocopied   Practical 4: Enzymes

Background Knowledge

Required Practical 4

Task 4 Circle **three** organs on the diagram where **amylase** is made.

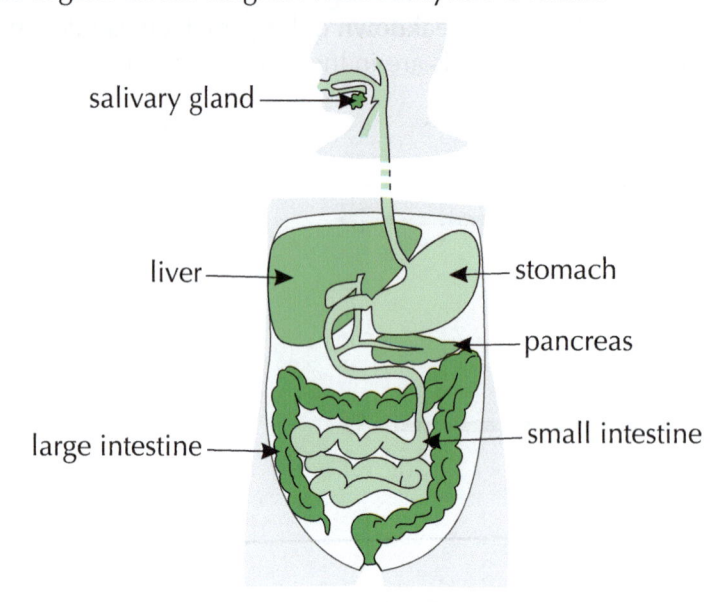

- salivary gland
- liver
- stomach
- pancreas
- large intestine
- small intestine

Task 5 On each set of axes below, **sketch a graph** to show how the variable affects the **rate** of enzyme activity. Draw a **cross** at the point on the graph that shows the **optimum** temperature or pH.

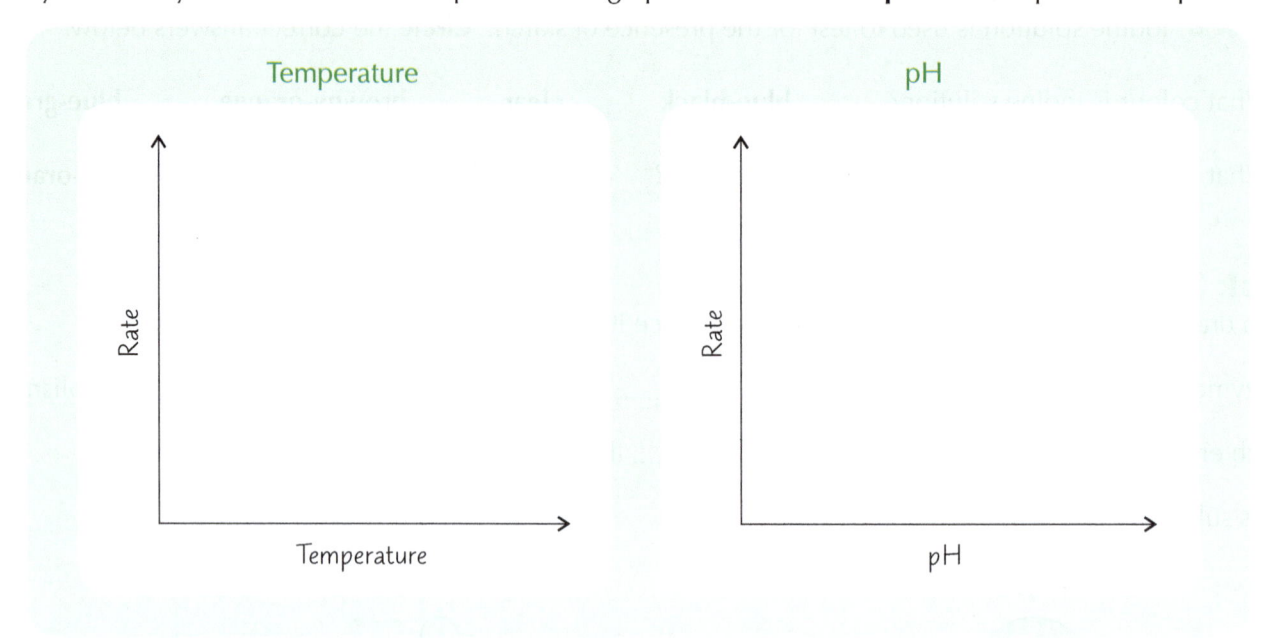

Temperature — Rate vs Temperature

pH — Rate vs pH

Explain what happens to an enzyme at a really high temperature or pH.

I don't like studying — I guess amalasey student...

DISCUSS Generally, increasing the concentration of a substance in a reaction will speed up the reaction rate. However, if you increase the amount of substrate in an enzyme-substrate reaction, the rate will only increase up to a point. Discuss with your partner why this is. What could you change to speed it up more?

Practical 4: Enzymes

Practical

Required Practical 4

Task 6 The steps to set up an experiment to investigate how **pH** affects **amylase** action are outlined below. Look at the procedure and diagrams to answer the questions.

Set Up Procedure

1. Put a drop of iodine solution into every well of a spotting tile.

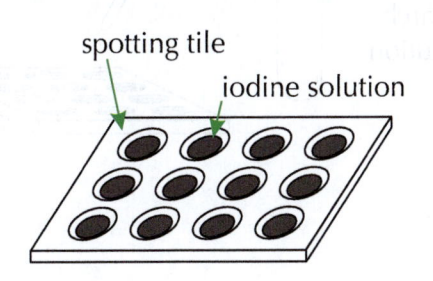

2. Set up a water bath using a Bunsen burner, tripod and beaker of water. Heat the water until it is 35 °C.

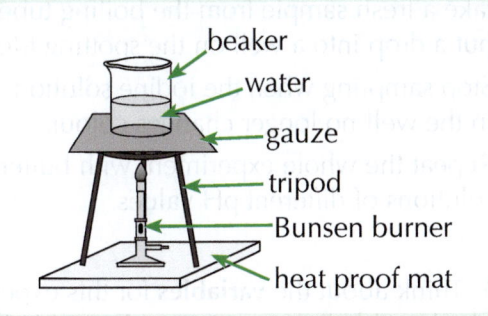

3. Use a syringe to add 1 cm³ of amylase solution and 1 cm³ of a buffer solution with a pH of 5 to a boiling tube.
4. Put the boiling tube into the water bath.
5. Add 5 cm³ of starch solution to another boiling tube and place this in the water bath. Leave both boiling tubes for five minutes.

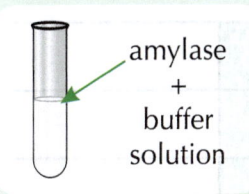

Key Definition
Buffer Solution
A solution that resists changes in pH.

Always use tongs when putting boiling tubes in the water bath.

Why do you think the temperature for the water bath is 35 °C?

....

Why are the boiling tubes left in the water bath for 5 minutes?

....

Name a piece of equipment you'll need for Step 2 that isn't shown in the diagram. ....

Think about what you need to measure in this step.

What could you use to measure the pH of the buffer solution? ....

Task 7 Can you think of any **hazards** in this experiment? How could you reduce any potential **risks** from them?

Key Definitions
Hazard
Something that has the potential to cause harm.
Risk
The chance that a hazard will cause harm.

© CGP — not to be photocopied

Practical 4: Enzymes

Required Practical 4 — Practical

Procedure

1. Add the starch solution to the boiling tube containing the amylase and buffer solution.
2. Immediately mix the contents of the boiling tube and start a stop clock.
3. At regular intervals, use a dropping pipette to take a fresh sample from the boiling tube and put a drop into a well on the spotting tile.
4. Stop sampling when the iodine solution in the well no longer changes colour.
5. Repeat the whole experiment with buffer solutions of different pH values.

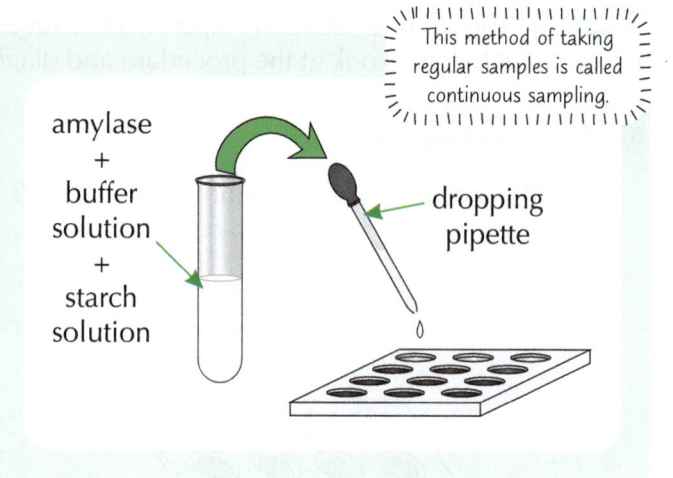

This method of taking regular samples is called continuous sampling.

Task 8 Think about the **variables** for this experiment. List them in the table below. A **control** variable has been added to get you started.

Independent Variable	
Dependent Variable	
Control Variables	Volume of starch,

Why should the **same volume** of starch solution be used for different pH tests?

....

....

Suggest how you could set up a **control test** for this experiment.

....

....

A control test should be kept under the same conditions as the rest of the investigation, but not have anything done to it.

Task 9 Write down a **hypothesis** for this experiment.

How much clock could a stop clock stop... (if a stop clock could stop clocks)

DISCUSS

Trypsin is an enzyme found in the small intestine that breaks down proteins. When added to milk, it breaks down the protein in the milk that makes it white, causing the milk to turn clear. This colour change can be observed by placing a dark piece of card behind a test tube in which the reaction is occurring. With a partner, use this information to come up with an experiment that you could do to find out the optimum temperature for trypsin. What would you measure? What variables would you need to control?

Practical 4: Enzymes

Results and Analysis

Required Practical 4

Task 10 A student carried out this experiment at **pH 6**, taking samples every **15 seconds**. The diagram below shows their spotting tile at the end of the experiment. The samples are numbered from 1 to 12.

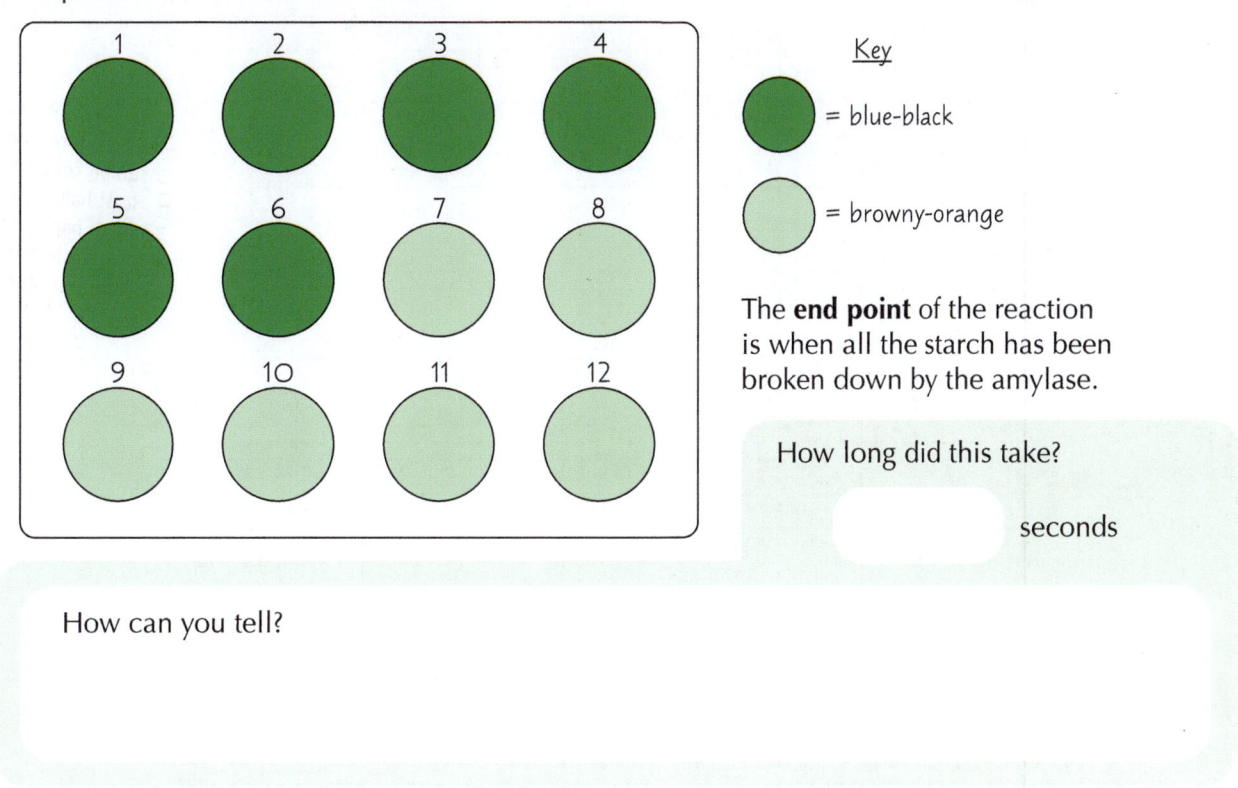

Key:
- ● = blue-black
- ○ = browny-orange

The **end point** of the reaction is when all the starch has been broken down by the amylase.

How long did this take? _____ seconds

How can you tell?

Task 11 The table below shows some **example results** for the time taken for amylase to break down starch at different pH levels. The **rate of reaction** can be calculated using this formula:

$$\text{rate} = \frac{1000}{\text{time (s)}}$$

Use the formula to complete the table. Give each rate of reaction to **1 decimal place**. The first row has been done for you.

pH of buffer solution	Time taken (s)	Rate of reaction (s^{-1})
4	270	3.7
5	210	
6	120	
7	90	
8	150	
9	480	

Practical 4: Enzymes

Results and Analysis

Required Practical 4

Task 12 Use the results from Task 11 to **plot a graph** to show the relationship between the pH and rate of reaction. Include a **line of best fit**.

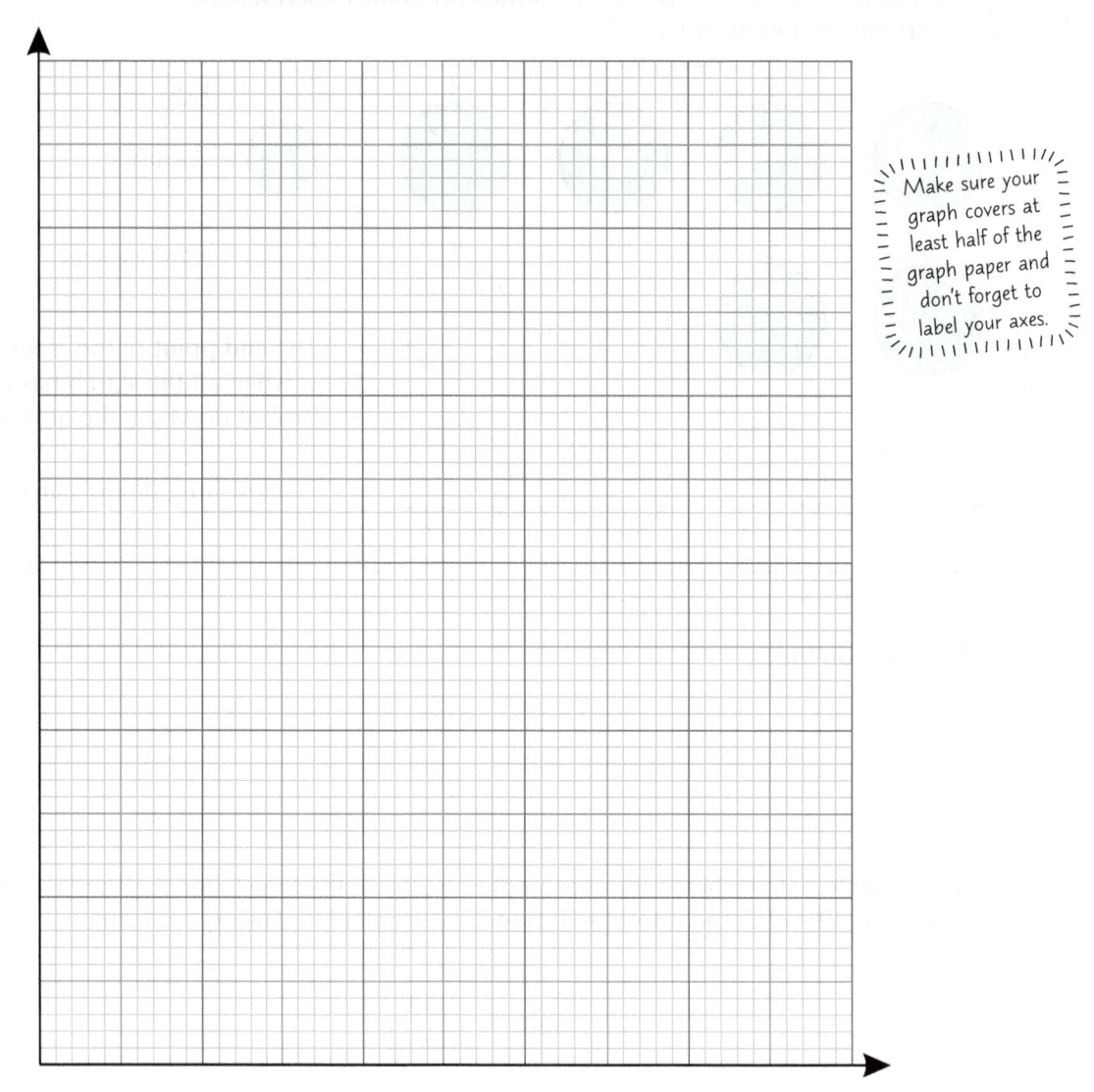

Make sure your graph covers at least half of the graph paper and don't forget to label your axes.

Task 13 Kyle followed the same method and got the following results. Circle the **anomalous** result in Kyle's table.

Key Definition
Anomalous result
A result that doesn't seem to fit with the rest of the data.

pH of buffer solution	Time taken (s)
4	300
5	630
6	150
7	120
8	150
9	450

Kyle worked out that the anomalous result was caused by a problem with the buffer solution. What should Kyle do with this result?

....

....

....

....

Practical 4: Enzymes

Conclusions and Evaluation

Required Practical 4

Task 14 What can you **conclude** from the graph you plotted for Task 12?

Describe the graph. What happens to the rate of the reaction as the pH increases?

....

....

What do you think is happening to cause the shape of the graph?

....

....

....

....

....

From these results, what can you conclude about the **optimum pH** for amylase? Explain your answer.

....

....

....

Task 15 Look back at the example results in Task 11. Think about how the method for this experiment could be **improved** to make those results more **accurate**. Write some notes in the box below.

Key Definition

Accurate result
A result that is very close to the true answer.

© CGP — not to be photocopied

Practical 4: Enzymes

| Required Practical 4 | # Conclusions and Evaluation |

Task 16 Desta carried out this practical by following a similar method to the one outlined on pages 27-28, but she found that it was difficult to gather results as the reaction was happening **too fast**. Fill in the mind map below with **changes** she could make to her method to make the reaction slower, then answer the questions below.

Ways to slow down the reaction between amylase and starch

Another student has noticed that Desta picks up the pipette to take a sample at each time point, rather than having the pipette ready at that time. How might this affect her results?

....

....

....

Desta is using the second hand on her watch to time the experiment. Why should she use a stop clock instead?

....

Task 17 Think about how you could alter the experiment to investigate the effect of **temperature** on the rate of amylase activity. Make some notes below. Include a **graph** of what you think the results will show, with a label showing your prediction for the **optimum temperature**.

I'm concluding you've had enough of enzymes by now...

A colorimeter is a piece of equipment that can be used to measure the amount of light that passes through a sample solution. It can tell you the percentage of light that passes through the sample. With a partner, think about how you could adapt the method on pages 27-28 to use a colorimeter. How could you tell the end-point? What difference do you think it will make to your results?

Practical 4: Enzymes

Exam-Style Questions

Required Practical 4

Task 18 Try these **exam-style** questions.

1 Pepsin is an enzyme found in the stomach that breaks down proteins. A scientist carried out an experiment to investigate optimum temperature for pepsin, following this method:

> 1) Add 5 cm³ egg white suspension to a test tube.
> 2) Add two drops of hydrochloric acid.
> 3) Add 1 cm³ of pepsin to a second test tube.
> 4) Place both test tubes in a water bath at 30 °C for 5 minutes.
> 5) Add the contents of the second test tube to the first test tube.
> 6) Hold the first test tube up to a light to observe the colour change.
> 7) Record the time taken for the colour change to occur (this is the end of the reaction).

The egg white suspension turns from white to clear as the pepsin breaks it down.

1.1 Suggest why hydrochloric acid is added to the first test tube.

....
[1]

Table 1 shows the scientist's results.

Table 1

Temperature (°C)	Time taken for colour change (s)				Mean rate of reaction (s⁻¹)
	Repeat 1	Repeat 2	Repeat 3	Mean	
30	126	84	90	100	
40	89	65	86	80	
50	118	125	X	125	
60	511	526	463	500	

1.2 Calculate the value of X in the table.

.... s
[1]

1.3 Complete the table by calculating the rate of reaction at each temperature.
Use the formula: rate = 1000 ÷ time

[2]

1.4 Explain a source of error in the scientist's method and suggest how to improve it.

....

....
[2]

1.5 Suggest why the scientist might want to repeat the experiment again at 30 °C and 40 °C.

....
[1]

[Total 7 marks]

Practical 5: Photosynthesis

Required Practical 5

Background Knowledge

If you've ever wondered why plants grow faster when the sun shines, you're in luck. In this practical you will investigate the effect of **light intensity** on the **rate** of **photosynthesis**. First up, a little theory.

Task 1 **Fill in the gaps** to complete these sentences about photosynthesis.

Photosynthesis takes place in the .... in green plant cells. Energy from light is transferred to them and used to make .... for the plant. The reaction is described as .... because energy is transferred from the environment to the plant.

Task 2 Complete the **word equation** for photosynthesis. Then look at the chemical symbols in the box below and write them in the correct places to complete the **symbol equation**.

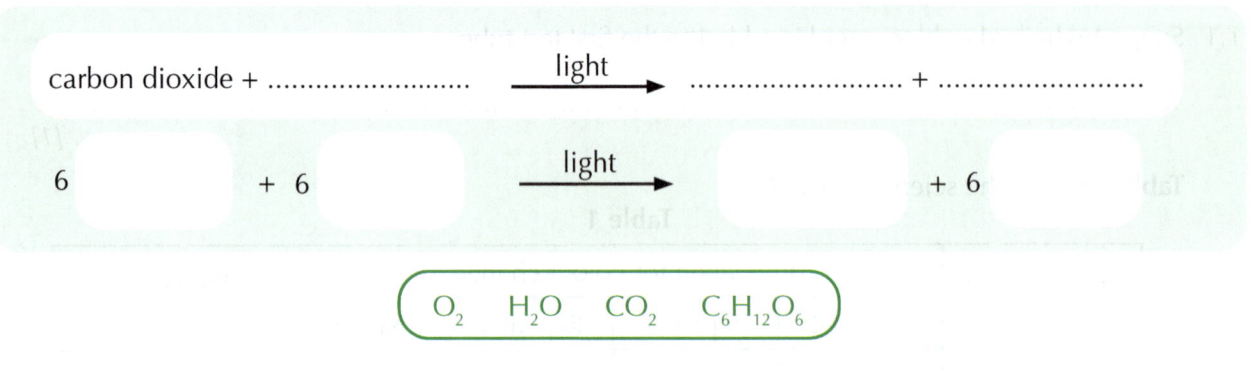

carbon dioxide + ... $\xrightarrow{\text{light}}$ .... + ...

6 .... + 6 .... $\xrightarrow{\text{light}}$ .... + 6 ....

O_2 H_2O CO_2 $C_6H_{12}O_6$

Task 3 The **rate** of photosynthesis is affected by light intensity, carbon dioxide concentration and temperature. Any one of these can become a **limiting factor**. The graph below shows the effect of **light intensity** on the rate of photosynthesis.

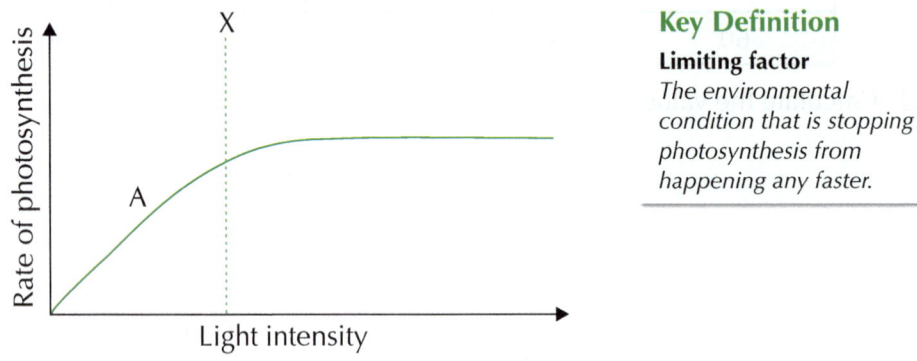

Key Definition
Limiting factor
The environmental condition that is stopping photosynthesis from happening any faster.

What is happening in the part of the graph labelled A?

Why does the shape of the graph change after the line labelled X?

Background Knowledge

Required Practical 5

Task 4 Look at the graphs below showing how **carbon dioxide** and **temperature** affect the rate of photosynthesis. Add a **label** to the **x-axis** of each. Write the **correct letter** for each label on the graph.

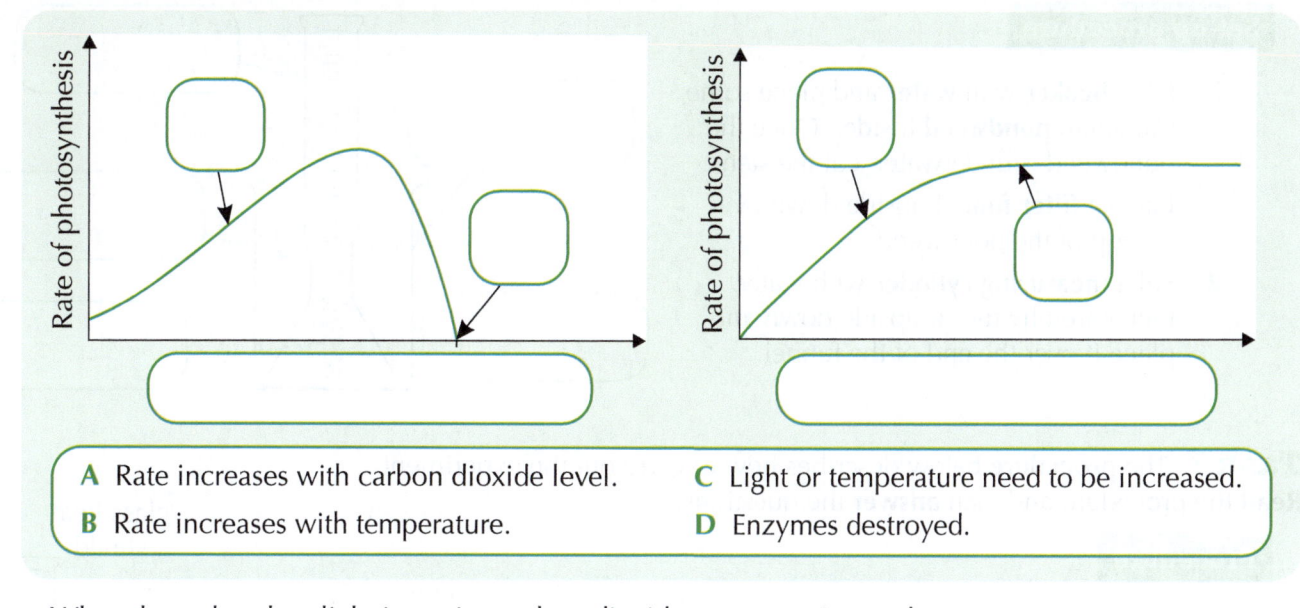

A Rate increases with carbon dioxide level.
B Rate increases with temperature.
C Light or temperature need to be increased.
D Enzymes destroyed.

What else, other than light intensity, carbon dioxide concentration and temperature, can affect the rate of photosynthesis?

....

Task 5 The graph below shows how photosynthesis is affected by **light intensity** and **temperature**.

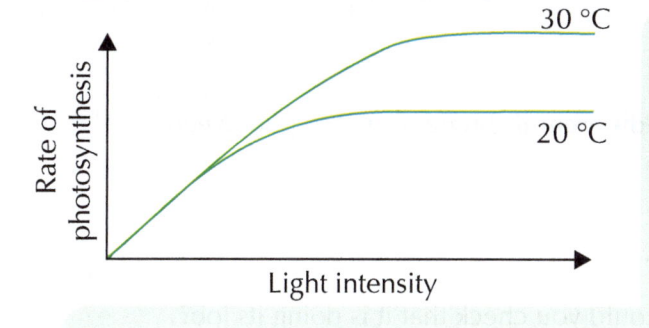

Explain the difference between the two lines on the graph.

Sketch a line on the graph to show how the rate of photosynthesis would change at 25 °C.

Why does **temperature** affect the rate of photosynthesis?

....
....
....

I can just tell this practical is going to be de-light-ful...

DISCUSS Limiting factors don't stay the same. With a partner, think of some examples of changes in the environment that would change the limiting factor. How might disease affect the rate of photosynthesis?

© CGP — not to be photocopied

Practical 5: Photosynthesis

Required Practical 5 — Practical

Task 6 Read the **set-up procedure** below for investigating the effect of **light intensity** on the **rate of photosynthesis**. Then label the diagram using the words in **bold** in the procedure.

Set-up procedure

1. Fill a **beaker** with **water** and place some Canadian **pondweed** inside. Once the pondweed is underwater, cut the stem.
2. Place a **filter funnel** upside down over the top of the pondweed.
3. Fill a **measuring cylinder** with water, then carefully turn it upside down and place it over the end of the funnel.

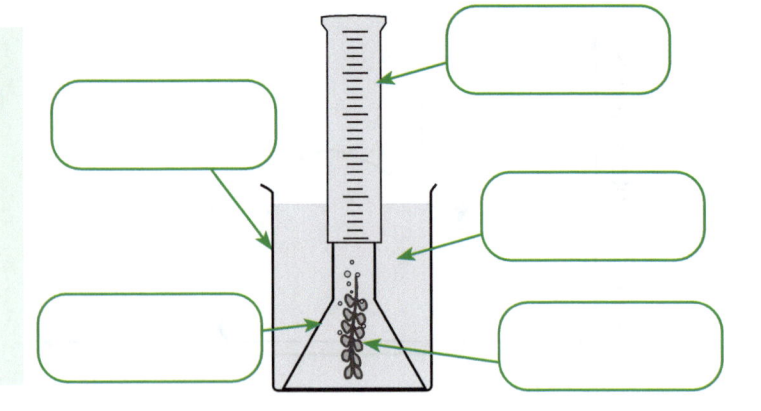

Task 7 The **procedure** below describes how to carry out the experiment. **Read** the procedure and then **answer** the questions.

Procedure

1. Place a source of white light at a **set distance** from the pondweed.
2. Place a glass **heat shield** between the light and beaker.
3. **Leave** the set-up for a few minutes.
4. When ready, **count** the bubbles produced from the cut end of the pondweed within a set amount of time.
5. After the set time, **measure** the **volume of gas** collected in the measuring cylinder.
6. Repeat the experiment with the light source at **different distances** from the pondweed in order to vary the light intensity.

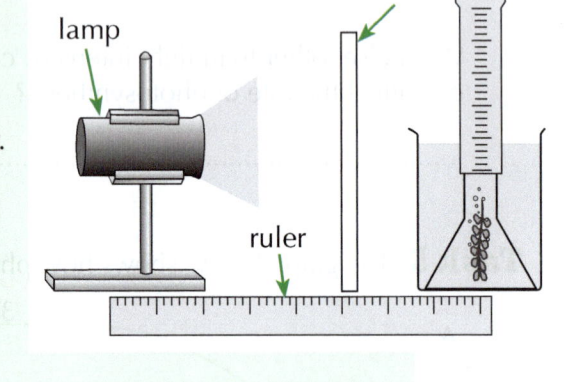

What is the gas that is being collected? ....

What is the purpose of the glass heat shield? How could you check that it is doing its job?

....

....

....

Why do you need to wait a few minutes, as described in step 3, at each new light intensity?

....

Would it be better to use the same plant or a different plant each time you repeat the experiment with the light source at different distances? Why?

....

....

....

Practical 5: Photosynthesis © CGP — not to be photocopied

Practical

Required Practical 5

Task 8 The **rate** of photosynthesis can be measured by **counting the bubbles** produced from the cut end of the pondweed or by **measuring the volume** of oxygen produced. In the boxes below, comment on the **accuracy** of the results produced by each of these methods.

Counting bubbles:

Measuring the volume of oxygen:

Key Definition
Accuracy
How close to the true answer the results are.

Task 9 Two different students are trying to set up the experiment so that the light source is 40 cm from the pondweed. **Annotate** the diagrams of their set-ups to show any **sources of error** you can see.

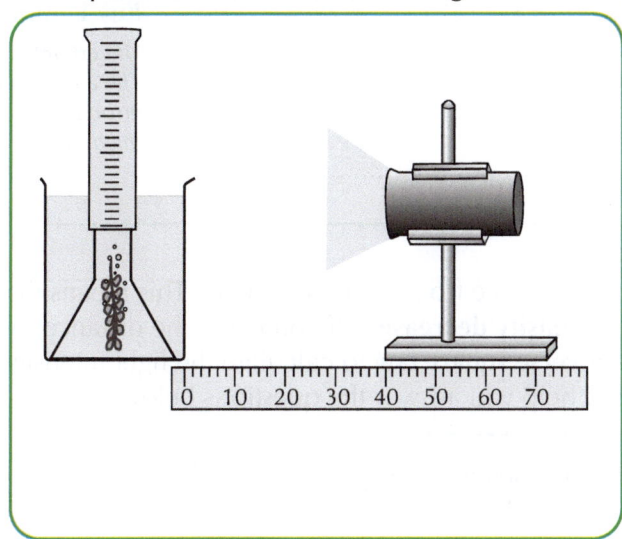

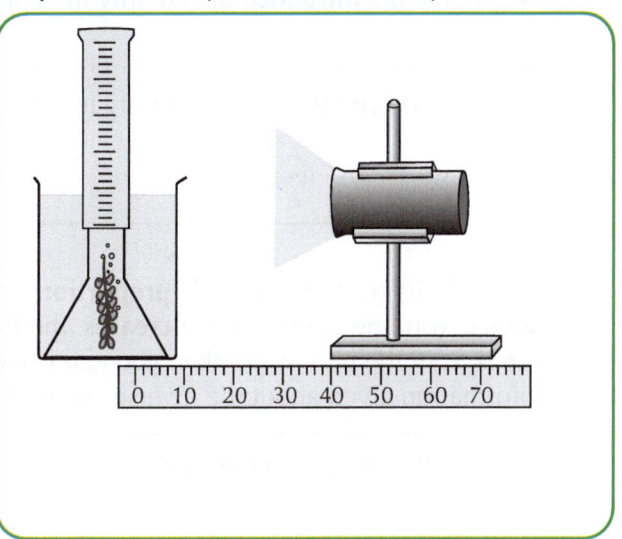

Task 10 Complete the sentences below about **safety** and **ethical** considerations for this practical.

Key Definition
Ethical considerations
Factors relating to whether or not something is morally right or wrong.

Safety considerations

There is a risk of infection from the pondwater so you should ....
....
Handling water near electricity can be dangerous so you should ....
....

Ethical considerations

You should dispose of the pondweed carefully after the experiment because ....
....
....

Watch out for pond water — it's where the pond weed...

If the beaker of water you use is large enough, you don't need to use a glass heat shield. Discuss why you think this is with a partner. LED bulbs are much more energy efficient than halogen bulbs. Do you think you need to use a heat shield if you used an LED bulb in this experiment? Why or why not?

© CGP — not to be photocopied

Practical 5: Photosynthesis

Required Practical 5: Results and Analysis

Task 11 The **volume of gas** collected by a student carrying out the experiment is shown below. Calculate the **mean** and **range** for each distance. Round your answer to **1 decimal place**.

Distance (m)	Volume of gas collected (cm³) Repeat 1	Repeat 2	Repeat 3	Mean (cm³)	Range (cm³)	Uncertainty
0.2	1.2	1.3	1.6			
0.4	0.8	0.6	1.2			
0.6	0.5	0.3	0.6			

Use your results to **calculate** the **uncertainty** for the mean result at each distance. Give your answer to **2 decimal places**.

$$\text{Uncertainty} = \frac{\text{range}}{2}$$

What two factors **introduce** uncertainty in results?

....

How could you **reduce** the uncertainty in the experiment?

....

Key Definition
Uncertainty
The amount of error the results might have.

Task 12 Light intensity is **inversely proportional** to the distance from the light source. This means that as the **distance** from the light source **increases**, the **light intensity decreases**. If you know the distance the light source is from the pondweed then you can use the **inverse square law** to calculate the light intensity. Use the information given about the inverse square law to help you answer the questions below.

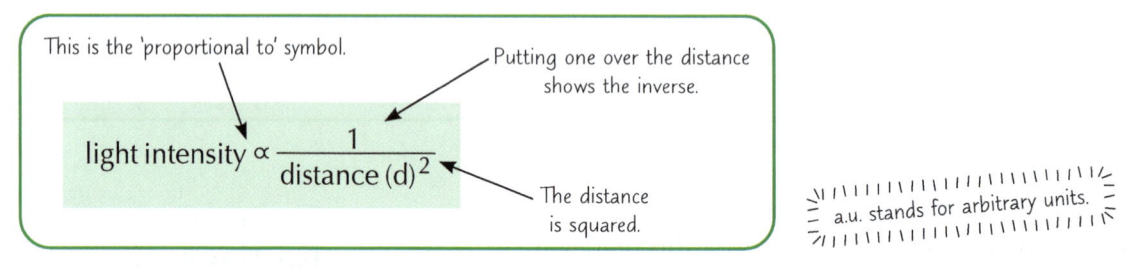

This is the 'proportional to' symbol. → ∝
Putting one over the distance shows the inverse.

$$\text{light intensity} \propto \frac{1}{\text{distance (d)}^2}$$

The distance is squared.

a.u. stands for arbitrary units.

So, in the experiment, if the lamp is 10 cm away, the light intensity is $\frac{1}{10^2} = \frac{1}{100} = 0.01$ a.u.

...if the lamp is 5 cm away, the light intensity is $\frac{1}{5^2} = \frac{1}{25} = 0.04$ a.u.

...if the lamp is 20 cm away, the light intensity is $\frac{1}{20^2} = \frac{1}{400} = 0.0025$ a.u.

What happens to the light intensity if the **distance** is **doubled**? Circle the correct answer.

- Light intensity is 1/2 of what it was.
- Light intensity is 1/8 of what it was.
- Light intensity is 1/4 of what it was.

What happens to the light intensity if the **distance** is **halved**? Circle the correct answer.

- Light intensity is 2 times what it was.
- Light intensity is 4 times what it was.
- Light intensity is 8 times what it was.

Practical 5: Photosynthesis

Results and Analysis

Required Practical 5

Task 13 The **mean volume of gas** collected by another student during the experiment is shown below. The gas was collected over a period of **10 minutes**. **Complete** the table.

Distance from light source (m)	Light intensity (arbitrary units)	Mean volume of gas (cm³)	Rate (cm³/min)
0.20	25.0	2.6	0.26
0.40		2.0	
0.60		1.2	
0.80		1.6	
1.00		0.6	

Calculate the light intensity at each distance using the inverse square law.

Calculate the rate by dividing the volume of gas given off by the time.

Task 14 Use the results above to **plot a graph** of light intensity against rate. Draw a **line of best fit**.

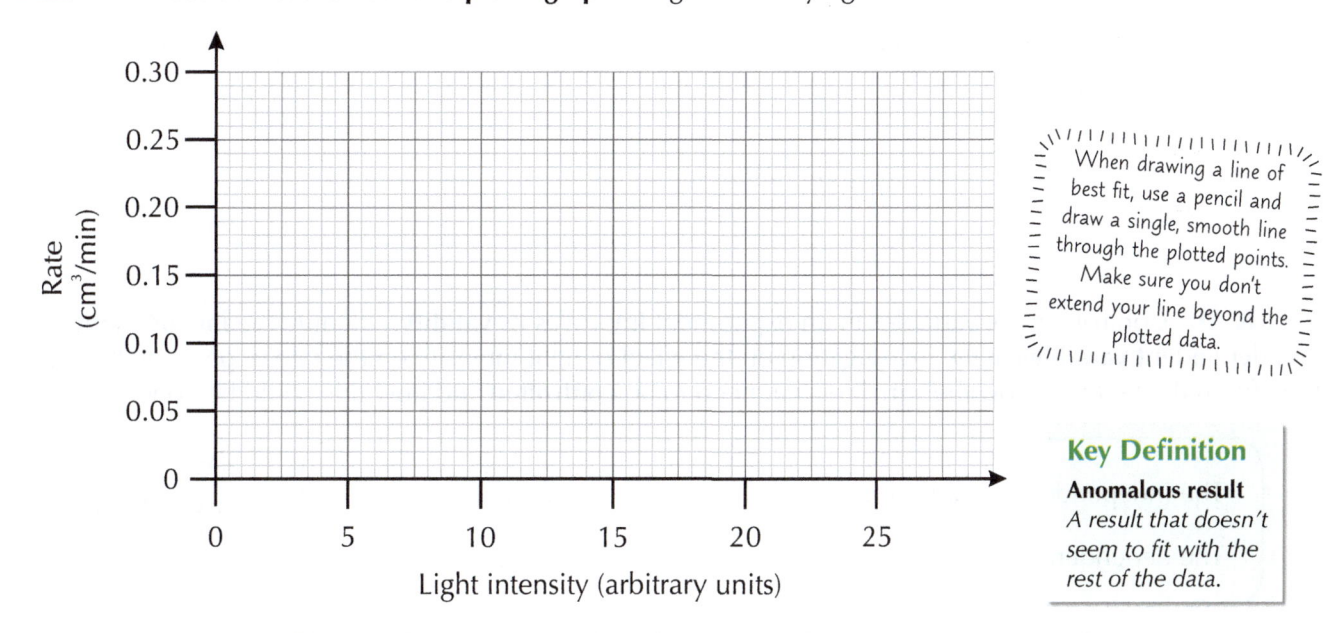

When drawing a line of best fit, use a pencil and draw a single, smooth line through the plotted points. Make sure you don't extend your line beyond the plotted data.

Key Definition
Anomalous result
A result that doesn't seem to fit with the rest of the data.

Circle the **anomalous** result.

When can you discount an anomalous result? Give an example for this experiment.

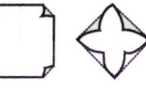

....

....

DISCUSS — inverse squares make me so cross...

Draw a lamp with light rays coming from it. Use your diagram to discuss with a partner why light intensity is inversely proportional to distance squared. Why inverse? And why square the distance?

© CGP — not to be photocopied

Practical 5: Photosynthesis

Conclusions and Evaluation

Required Practical 5

Task 15 Look at the results on the previous page. What **conclusions** can you draw? Fill in the **missing words** and **answer** the questions below.

Initially, as light intensity ...., the rate of photosynthesis ....

At light intensities above .... the rate of photosynthesis levels off.

Can you explain the shape of the graph? Which factor is limiting the rate of photosynthesis at the start of the experiment? Why does it level off?

....

....

....

....

What changes would stop the graph levelling off?

Think about what the limiting factors must be.

....

....

Task 16 Controlling the variables in an experiment improves its **validity**. Identify the **independent** and **dependent variables** in the investigation on the effect of light intensity on the rate of photosynthesis, then fill in the table to show the variables that need to be **controlled** and how this could be done.

The independent variable was ....

The dependent variable was ....

Key Definitions

Independent variable
The variable in an experiment that is changed.

Dependent variable
The variable in an experiment that is measured.

Control variable
A variable in an experiment that is kept the same.

Variables to control	How to control the variable

Hint: adding sodium hydrogencarbonate to water provides a source of carbon dioxide.

Practical 5: Photosynthesis

Conclusions and Evaluation

Required Practical 5

Task 17 When investigating the effect of light intensity on the rate of photosynthesis, how could you increase the **reliability** of the results?

....

....

....

> **Key Definition**
> **Reliable results**
> *Results that are repeatable and reproducible.*

Task 18 A student wants to investigate the effect of **temperature** and **carbon dioxide** on the rate of photosynthesis. Fill in the boxes below to show how the experiment could be adapted to investigate these.

Temperature	Carbon dioxide concentration
Outline of change to method	*Outline of change to method*

Task 19 The experiment can also be carried out using a **gas syringe**, rather than collecting the gas in the upturned measuring cylinder. At the end of the experiment the gas syringe is used to draw the oxygen bubble into the capillary tube as shown below and the **length** of the bubble is measured.

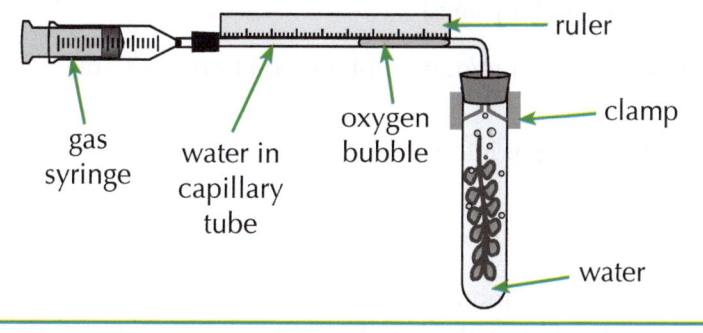

Which apparatus do you think would produce the more **accurate** results — the gas syringe or the upturned measuring cylinder? Why?

DISCUSS

Temperature increases rate — it's not just hot air...

Discuss with a partner the potential commercial benefits of investigating the rate of photosynthesis and the factors that limit it. How could growers put the theory into practice to increase their profits?

Required Practical 5 — **Exam-Style Questions**

Task 20 Try these **exam-style** questions.

1   A student used the apparatus below to investigate the effect of light intensity on the rate of photosynthesis. The student measured the length of the oxygen bubble produced in 3 minutes.

1.1   Write down the length of the oxygen bubble.

.... mm
[1]

1.2   Calculate the rate of photosynthesis at this light intensity. Give your answer in mm/min to 1 s.f.

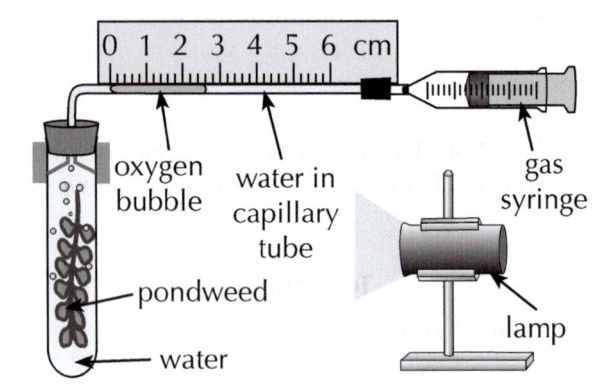

.... mm/min
[1]

1.3   The student plots the results of the experiment on the graph below.

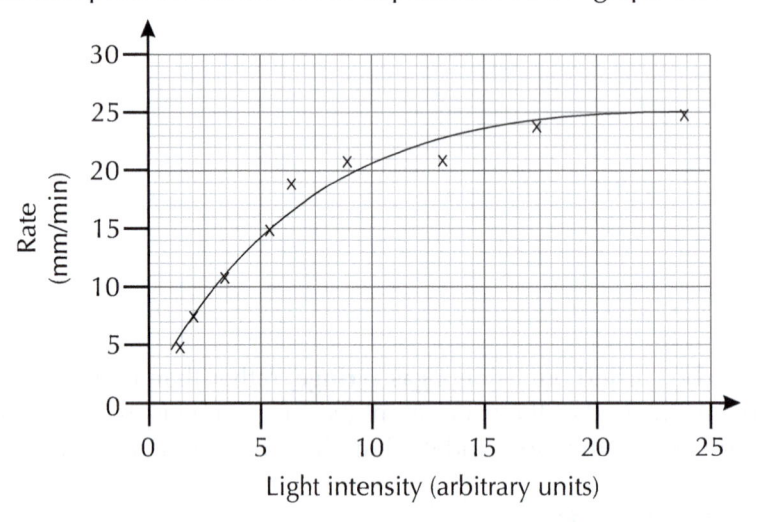

At a light intensity of 15 a.u., the rate was 25 mm/min. Plot the point on the graph.
[1]

1.4   What would you expect the rate to be at a light intensity of 5 a.u.?

.... mm/min
[1]

1.5   The student conducted the experiment in the laboratory with the window blinds open. Explain why leaving the blinds open would have affected the validity of the experiment.

....

....
[2]

1.6   Give one possible source of systematic error in the experiment.

....

....
[1]

[Total 7 marks]

Practical 5: Photosynthesis   © CGP — not to be photocopied

Practical 6: Reaction Time

Background Knowledge

Required Practical 6

This practical is about **reaction time**. You will work with a partner to investigate the effect of one **factor** on the **speed** at which you can catch a ruler being dropped. Time to get competitive.

Task 1 Fill in the blanks to complete the definition of the **central nervous system (CNS)**:

The CNS consists of the brain and _____.

It is connected to the body by _____ neurones and _____ neurones.

It is where reflexes and actions are _____.

Task 2 Draw lines to match up the **following terms** with their **definitions**.

Stimulus — Either a muscle or gland that responds to nervous impulses.

Receptor — A change in the environment.

Effector — A cell which is sensitive to a stimulus.

Task 3 Complete the sentences below by circling the **correct option** in each set of brackets.

Sensory neurones carry impulses from receptors to (**the CNS** / motor neurones).

Motor neurones carry impulses from (sensory neurones / **the CNS**) to the (**effectors** / stimulus).

Relay neurones carry impulses from (motor / **sensory**) neurones to (**motor** / sensory) neurones.

Task 4 The flow chart below shows the transmission of information to and from the CNS. Circle the two components of the nervous system that are in the **wrong order**.

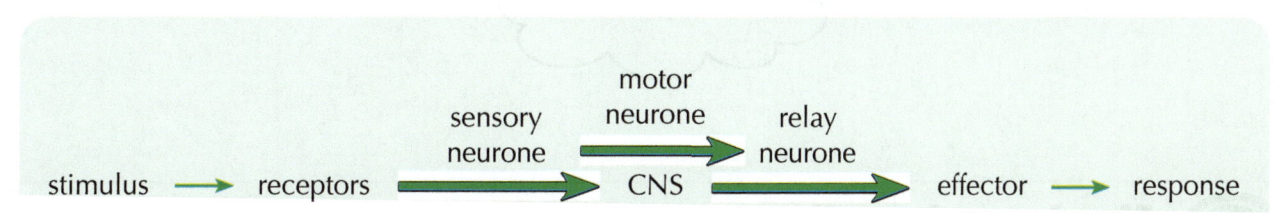

stimulus → receptors → sensory neurone → motor neurone → CNS → relay neurone → effector → response

© CGP — not to be photocopied

Practical 6: Reaction Time

Required Practical 6: Background Knowledge

Task 5 Some nervous system responses go via the conscious brain. **Reflexes**, on the other hand, bypass the conscious part of the brain when a quick response to a stimulus is needed. Why might you need to respond to a stimulus **quickly**?

....

Tick the scenarios below that are examples of **reflex responses**.

Scenario	Reflex
Suddenly moving your hand away from a sharp object.	☐
Blinking when a bright light is shone in your face.	☐
Moving away from a hole in the ground.	☐
Catching a ball thrown at you unexpectedly.	☐
Dropping a hot pan.	☐

Imagine these things happening to you — do you think you'd respond with or without thinking about it first?

Task 6 **Synapses** are the connections between two neurones. They limit and control impulse transmission. On the diagram of the synapse below, draw an arrow to show the **direction** the nerve impulse is travelling in.

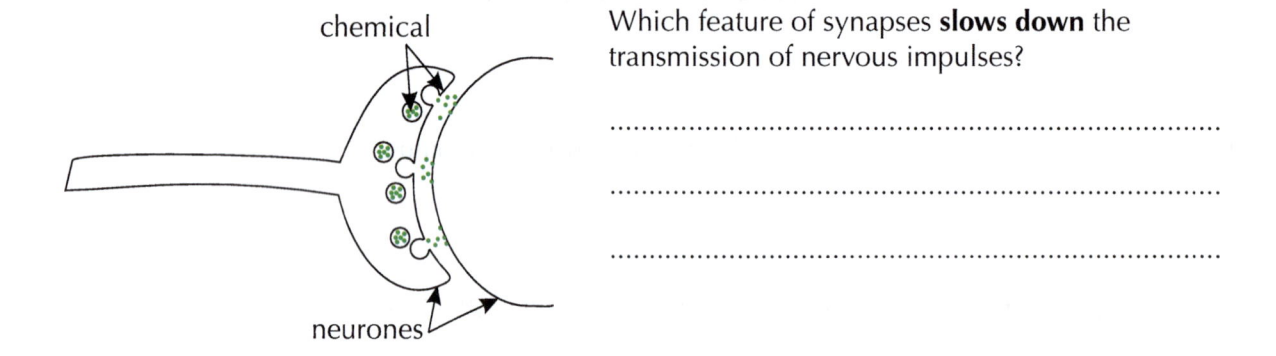

(diagram labelled: chemical, neurones)

Which feature of synapses **slows down** the transmission of nervous impulses?

....
....
....

Task 7 Look at the mind map below. Add some **factors** that affect reaction time.

(cloud: Factors affecting reaction time)

Key Definition
Reaction time
The time it takes to respond to a stimulus. This depends on the speed at which a message travels from the receptor to the effector, via the central nervous system.

DISCUSS — **If only my broadband was as fast as the CNS…**
Take a look at the factors affecting reaction time that you added to the mind map in Task 7. With a partner, discuss how you think these factors might affect reaction time and the reasons why.

Practical

Required Practical 6

Task 8 The effect of **caffeine** on reaction time can be investigated in pairs using the **ruler drop method**. This is where the 'participant' catches a ruler released by the 'dropper'. The **procedure** for this experiment is shown below, but the steps have been mixed up. Put the steps in the correct order (one has been done for you), then identify the **independent** and **dependent variables**.

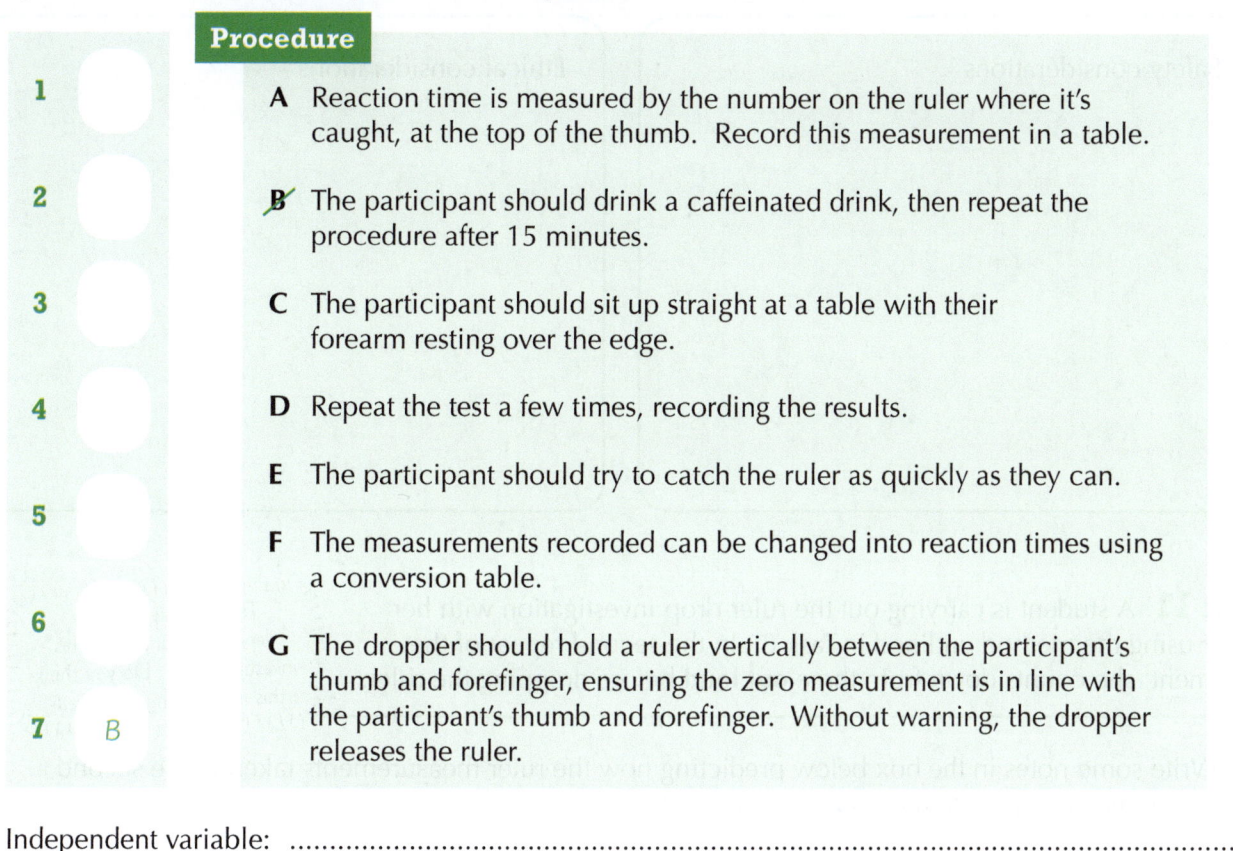

Procedure

1. ◯
2. ◯
3. ◯
4. ◯
5. ◯
6. ◯
7. B

A Reaction time is measured by the number on the ruler where it's caught, at the top of the thumb. Record this measurement in a table.

B The participant should drink a caffeinated drink, then repeat the procedure after 15 minutes.

C The participant should sit up straight at a table with their forearm resting over the edge.

D Repeat the test a few times, recording the results.

E The participant should try to catch the ruler as quickly as they can.

F The measurements recorded can be changed into reaction times using a conversion table.

G The dropper should hold a ruler vertically between the participant's thumb and forefinger, ensuring the zero measurement is in line with the participant's thumb and forefinger. Without warning, the dropper releases the ruler.

Independent variable: ....

Dependent variable: ....

Task 9 The diagrams below show the **ruler positions** before the ruler drop and the measurements taken after the ruler drop during three repeats.

Circle the diagram of the repeat that shows the steps being carried out correctly.

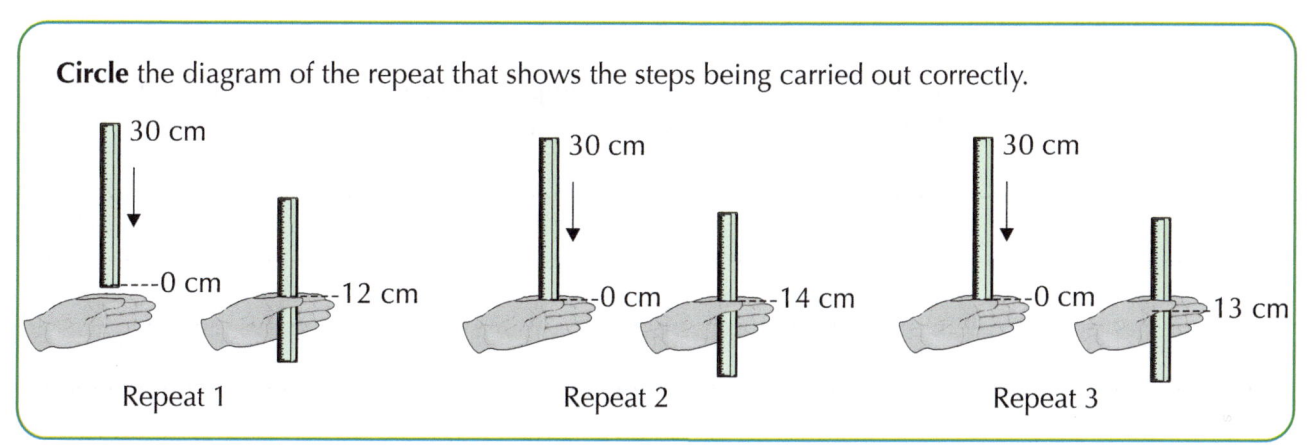

Repeat 1: 30 cm, 0 cm, 12 cm
Repeat 2: 30 cm, 0 cm, 14 cm
Repeat 3: 30 cm, 0 cm, 13 cm

For the repeats above that you **didn't circle**, note down the **problem** with each one.

Practical 6: Reaction Time

| Required Practical 6 | **Practical** |

Task 10 In the boxes below, list some **safety** and **ethical considerations** that you would need to take into account when investigating the effect of consuming a caffeinated drink on reaction time.

Key Definition
Ethical considerations
Factors relating to whether or not something is morally right or wrong.

Safety considerations

Ethical considerations

Task 11 A student is carrying out the ruler drop investigation with her partner using the method outlined in Task 8. In the second repeat of the experiment, she counts down from three **out loud** before dropping the ruler.

Think about what the dependent variable in this investigation is. Do you think this is still being measured?

Write some notes in the box below predicting how the ruler measurements taken in the second repeat may compare to those taken in the first repeat.

Task 12 A student wants to investigate whether room **temperature** has an effect on reaction time. Suggest how you could **adapt the procedure** in Task 8 to investigate this.

....
....
....
....
....

DISCUSS

Danger! Falling objects!
Okay, it's only a ruler being dropped by a short height, but you can never be too careful. Safety and ethics are really important when carrying out experiments on humans or animals. With a partner, discuss how you might safely and ethically investigate the effect of fatigue on reaction time.

Practical 6: Reaction Time

Results and Analysis

Required Practical 6

Task 13 The table below shows the reaction times of three participants before and after consuming the same volume of caffeine in a drink. Which participant's **data set** for the 'before' condition is the **least precise**? Write your answer in the box below and explain why.

Key Definition
Precise result
A result that is very close to the mean.

Repeat	Reaction time (s)					
	Participant 1		Participant 2		Participant 3	
	Before	After	Before	After	Before	After
1	0.19	0.09	0.24	0.15	0.20	0.10
2	0.18	0.11	0.13	0.16	0.18	0.09
3	0.21	0.12	0.23	0.16	0.19	0.11
Mean	0.19	0.11	0.20	0.16	0.19	0.10

The 'before' data set for participant .... is the least precise because

Task 14 Using the results in Task 13, draw a **bar chart** on the grid showing the mean reaction times of each participant before and after consuming the caffeinated drink. Make sure you complete the **key**.

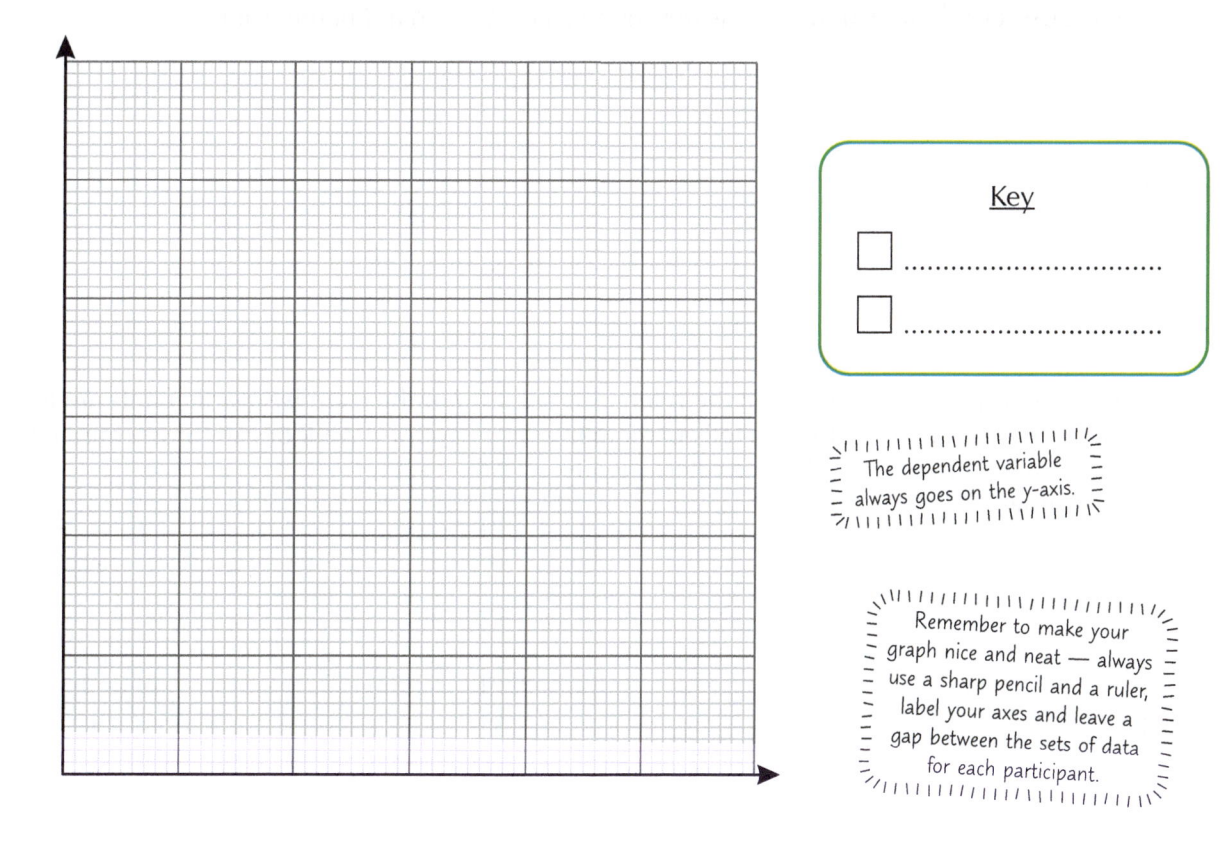

Key
☐ ....
☐ ....

The dependent variable always goes on the y-axis.

Remember to make your graph nice and neat — always use a sharp pencil and a ruler, label your axes and leave a gap between the sets of data for each participant.

Practical 6: Reaction Time

Required Practical 6

Conclusions and Evaluation

Task 15 What **conclusions** can you draw from the graph you drew in Task 14?

Task 16 A student investigates the effect of **age** on reaction time using the ruler drop method. He measures the reaction time of a group of six 12-year-olds and of a group of six 60-year-olds. Both groups have an even number of males and females and all other variables are controlled. Explain the **difficulty** that he might have in **drawing a conclusion** from his results.

....

....

....

....

....

Task 17 Esther and Brogan are working together to investigate the effect of **exercise** on **reaction time** using the ruler drop method and a group of volunteers. Each box below describes a different part of their method. In each box, jot down why the results may have been affected by their decisions.

Esther measures the participants' reaction time before exercise. After the participants have exercised, Brogan then measures the reaction time in a different room.

Esther tells participants to catch the ruler when they see it drop. Brogan tells participants to close their eyes and catch the ruler when he says 'now'.

For the exercise, participants are told to go for a walk or run for ten minutes.

Practical 6: Reaction Time © CGP — not to be photocopied

Exam-Style Questions

Required Practical 6

Task 18 Try these **exam-style** questions.

1   Student A is investigating the effect of a variable on reaction time.
    Their method is outlined below:
    1. In a silent room, hold a ruler between the thumb and forefinger of the participant.
    2. Drop the ruler without warning and record the distance the ruler falls before being caught.
    3. Repeat five times and calculate the mean distance.
    4. Repeat the experiment in a room with loud music playing.

1.1 Suggest a possible hypothesis that the student might have been collecting data to investigate.

    ....
    ....
    [1]

1.2 Give three variables that the student should control to ensure the investigation is a fair test.

    ....
    ....
    ....
    ....
    [3]

1.3 Reaction time from the ruler drop method can be calculated using the following formula:

$$\text{time (s)} = \sqrt{\text{mean distance (cm)} \div 490}$$

   The distances recorded by one participant are: 21.3 cm, 26.5 cm, 25.6 cm, 20.4 cm, 31.2 cm.
   Using the formula above, calculate the mean reaction time for the participant. Give your
   answer to 3 significant figures.

   .... seconds
   [2]

1.4 Student B also decides to investigate the effect of the same variable on reaction time using a
    computer programme. When the participant sees the screen turn red, they click the mouse
    and the reaction time is recorded by the computer. Student B tests the participants' reaction
    time five times in a silent room, and then again with loud music playing.

    Suggest and explain how the precision and accuracy of Student B's results will compare to
    Student A's results.

    ....
    ....
    ....
    ....
    [2]

    [Total 8 marks]

Practical 7: Field Investigations

Required Practical 7

Background Knowledge

This practical is all about investigating **how many** organisms there are in a habitat and **where you find them**. You can't post a census out to plants, so you have to **get outside** and have a look...

Task 1 Draw **lines** to match the key words to their definitions.

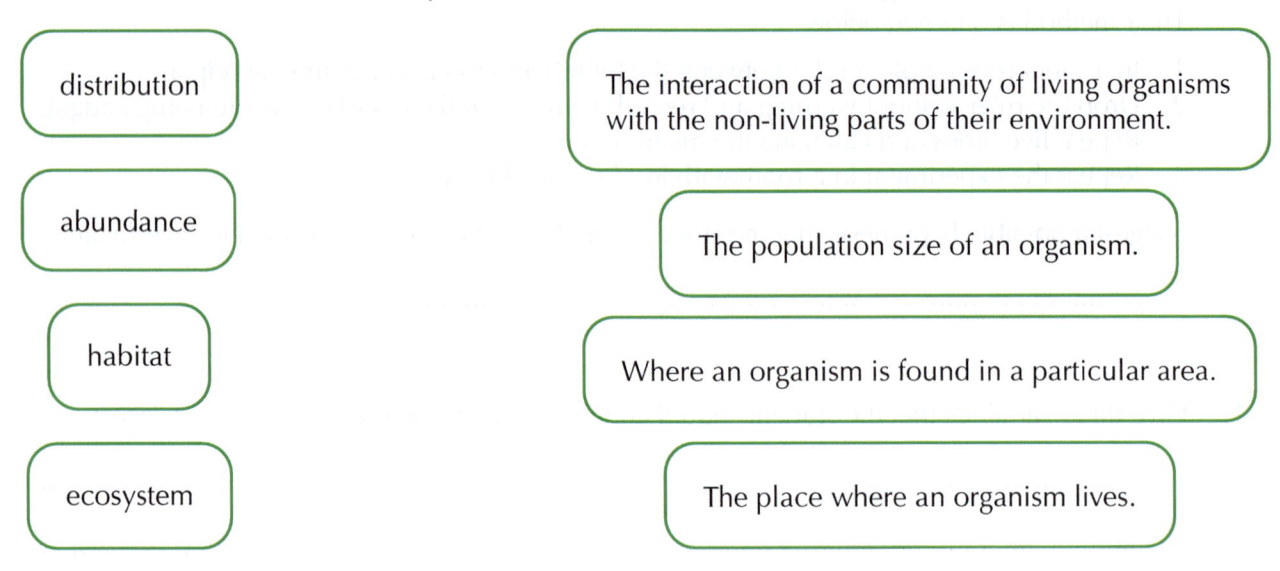

- distribution
- abundance
- habitat
- ecosystem

- The interaction of a community of living organisms with the non-living parts of their environment.
- The population size of an organism.
- Where an organism is found in a particular area.
- The place where an organism lives.

Task 2 Fill in this mind map to show the things that plants or animals **compete** for.

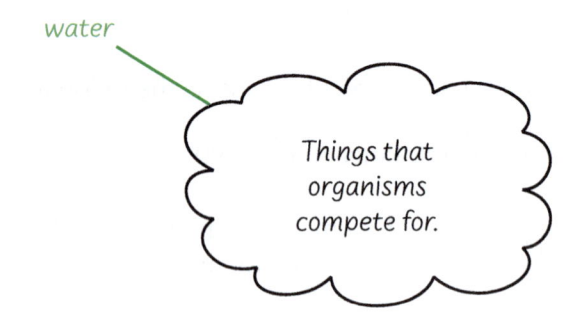

water — Things that organisms compete for.

Task 3 Tick the box to show whether these factors are **biotic** or **abiotic**.

	Biotic	Abiotic
Light intensity	☐	☐
New predator arriving	☐	☐
Soil pH	☐	☐
Carbon dioxide levels	☐	☐
New pathogen	☐	☐
Oxygen levels in water	☐	☐
Wind direction	☐	☐
Availability of food (for animals)	☐	☐
Temperature	☐	☐

Key Definitions
Abiotic factor
A non-living factor of the environment.
Biotic factor
A living factor of the environment.

Practical 7: Field Investigations

Background Knowledge

Required Practical 7

Task 4 Circle the graph below that shows a typical **predator-prey cycle**.

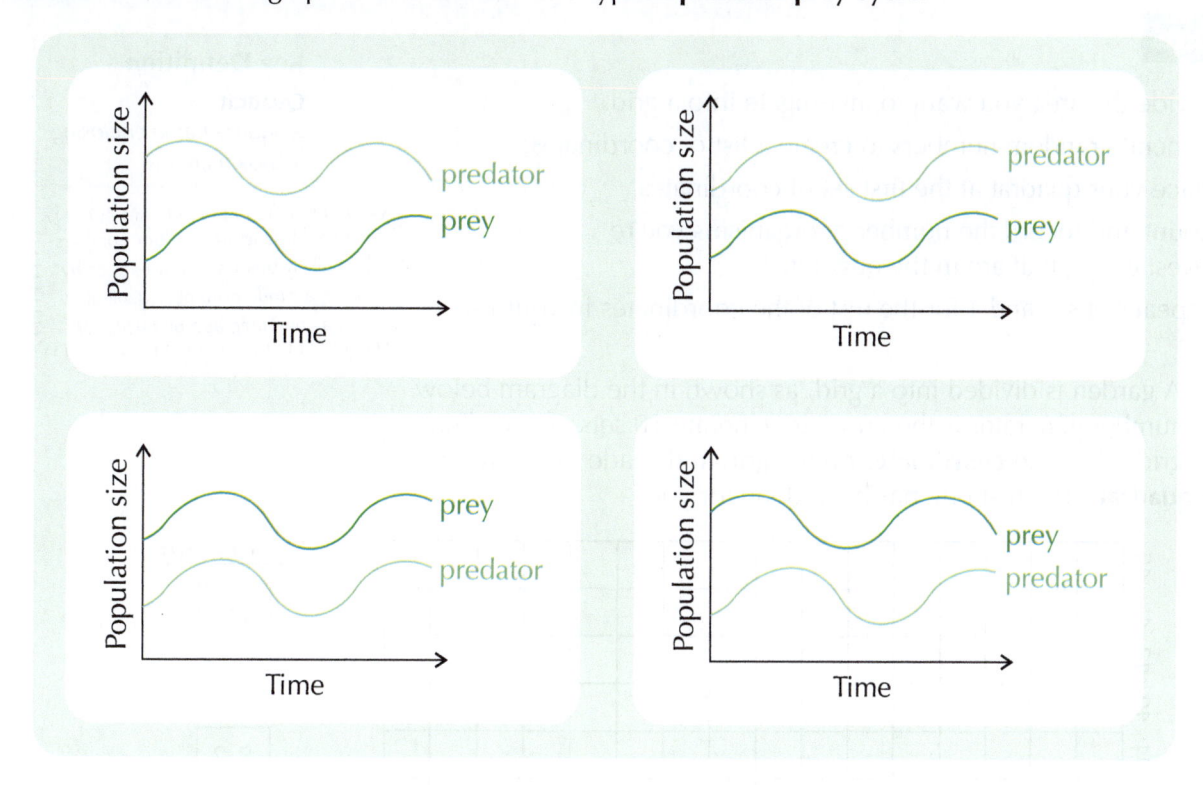

Task 5 Water voles live in burrows by rivers and ponds. They eat grasses and other plants at the water's edge. They have several predators, such as mink and owls.

The graph shows the change in a population of water voles over ten years.

Write down some **factors** that could explain the **change in population size** between **years 6** and **9**.

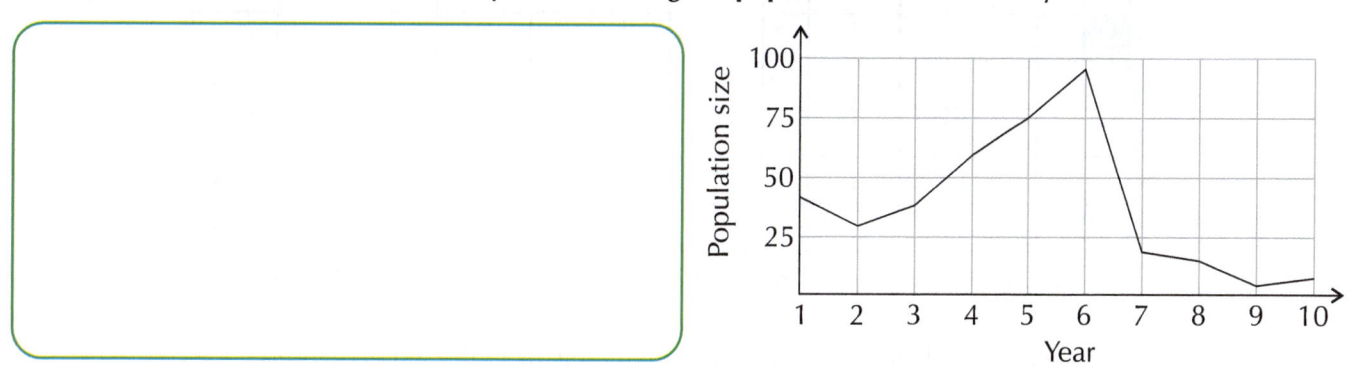

Task 6 Suggest a piece of equipment used to **measure** each of the following factors.

light intensity:

temperature:

soil pH:

Practical 7: Field Investigations

Required Practical 7 — Practical — Activity 1

The procedure below describes how to use a **quadrat** to investigate the **population size** of an organism.

Procedure

1. Divide the area you want to investigate into a grid.
2. Generate random numbers to create a list of coordinates.
3. Place your quadrat at the first set of coordinates.
4. Count and record the number of organisms you're investigating that are in the quadrat.
5. Repeat steps 3 and 4 for the rest of the coordinates in your list.

Key Definition
Quadrat
A square frame enclosing a known area.

You could generate random numbers by pulling them out of a bag, or by using a random number generator on a computer, app or calculator.

Task 7 A garden is divided into a grid, as shown in the diagram below. A random number generator is then used to generate 10 sets of coordinates within the grid. Find the **coordinates** on the grid and shade in where to **place the quadrat**. The first one has been done for you.

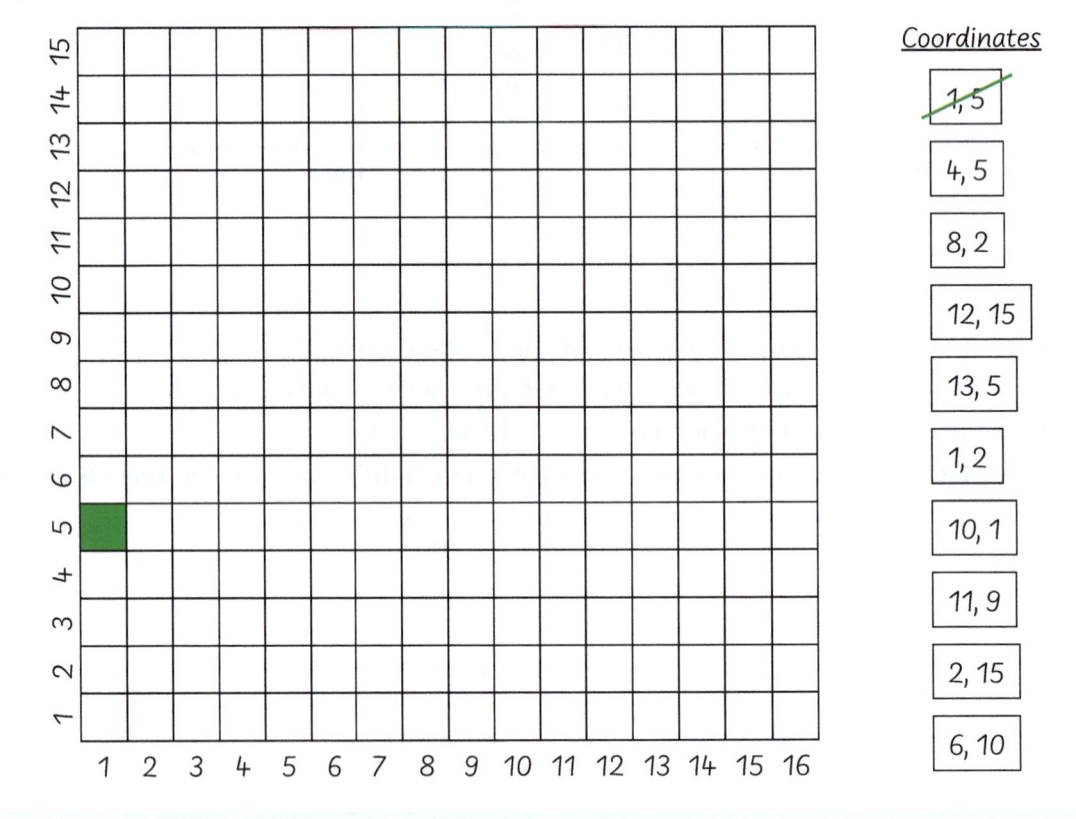

Coordinates:
- 1, 5 (done)
- 4, 5
- 8, 2
- 12, 15
- 13, 5
- 1, 2
- 10, 1
- 11, 9
- 2, 15
- 6, 10

Why are quadrats used, instead of counting all the organisms in the whole garden?

Why is using random coordinates better than choosing where to place each quadrat?

DISCUSS — It's like battleships, but with less fun and more rain...

With a partner, think about how you could adapt the procedure given on this page to compare the population size of one organism between two different areas, e.g. two halves of the same garden.

Practical 7: Field Investigations © CGP — not to be photocopied

Results and Analysis

Required Practical 7

Task 8 The **population size** of dandelions in the garden in Task 7 was investigated. Use the table of results to answer the following questions.

Quadrat	1	2	3	4	5	6	7	8	9	10
Number of dandelions	4	1	3	2	3	5	0	7	5	3

What is the **median** number of dandelions per quadrat?

....

What is the **mode** of this data set?

....

What is the **mean** number of dandelions per quadrat?

....

Key Definitions
Median
The value lying in the middle of a data set when the data is arranged in numerical order.
Mode
The number that appears most often in a data set.

The quadrat used had these dimensions: 0.5 m × 0.5 m

What was the total area sampled?

Think about the area of the quadrat and the number of samples taken.

....

Task 9 The garden being investigated in Task 7 is 8.0 metres long and 7.5 metres wide. Estimate the **population size** of dandelions in the garden using this equation:

$$\text{population size} = \frac{\text{total area being investigated (m}^2\text{)}}{\text{total area sampled (m}^2\text{)}} \times \text{total number of organisms counted}$$

You can also calculate population size by multiplying the mean number of organisms per m² by the total area being investigated (in m²).

....

Practical 7: Field Investigations

| Required Practical 7 | **Practical — Activity 2** |

The procedure below describes how to use a **transect** to study how an organism is **distributed** in an area.

Procedure

1. Mark out a line in the area you want to study using a tape measure.
2. Collect data along the line — either count all the organisms you're investigating that touch the line or collect data by using quadrats.

If you use quadrats along a transect, they can either be placed next to each other along the line or at intervals.

Task 10 Harper is investigating the effect of **light intensity** on the **percentage cover** of moss on his lawn.

One side of his lawn is covered with trees and the other side is exposed to full daylight for most of the day. Harper has observed that there's more moss under the trees. The layout of his garden is shown in the diagram.

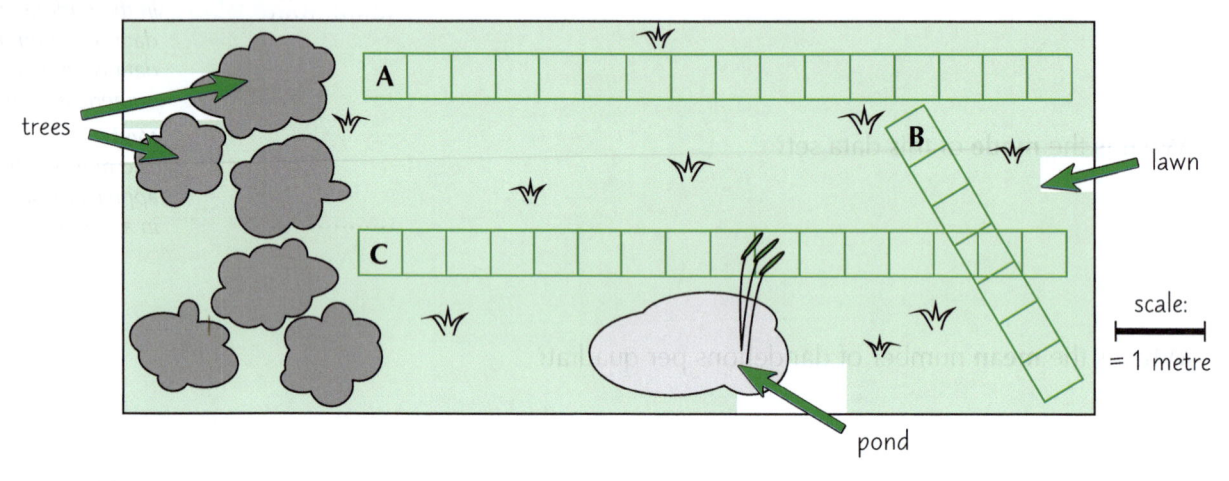

Harper plans to collect data by placing quadrats along a transect.

Which transect line on the diagram should he use for his investigation?

☐ A   ☐ B   ☐ C

Why have you chosen that transect?

Write a hypothesis for Harper's investigation.

Key Definition
Hypothesis
A possible explanation for a scientific observation.

Task 11 Give one **ethical consideration** that Harper should take into account during his investigation.

....

I prefer sampling across food markets...

DISCUSS Talk to a partner about how Harper should carry out his investigation. How often do you think he should take samples along the transect? Think about what else he should be measuring, and how he could measure it. Are there any hazards that he should be aware of? And what things might affect his results?

Practical 7: Field Investigations

Results and Analysis

Required Practical 7

Task 12 The diagram on the right shows the moss cover in one quadrat placed on Harper's lawn.

Percentage cover of an organism can be calculated using this equation:

$$\text{percentage cover} = \frac{\text{number of squares covered}}{\text{total number of squares}} \times 100$$

If a square is more than half covered, count it as covered.

◯ = moss

What is the percentage cover of moss in the quadrat?

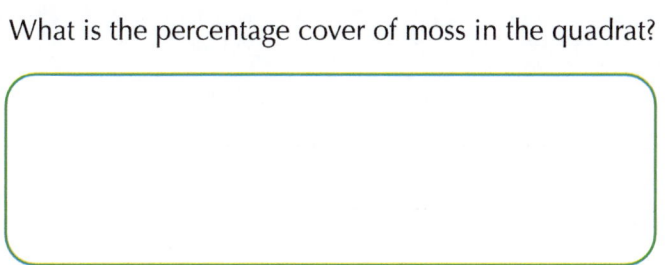

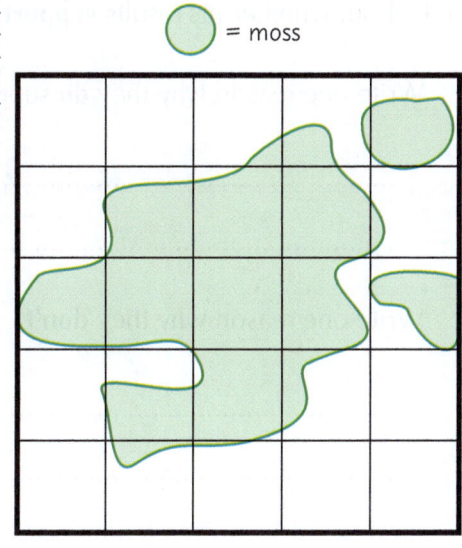

Task 13 Harper's results are shown in the table. Complete the graph below by **plotting** these results. Include a **key** for your graph.

Quadrat	1	2	3	4	5	6	7	8	9	10
Percentage cover (%)	4	10	13	22	35	24	47	56	60	78
Light intensity (× 10³ lux)	25	25	23	20	15	10	8	3	1	1

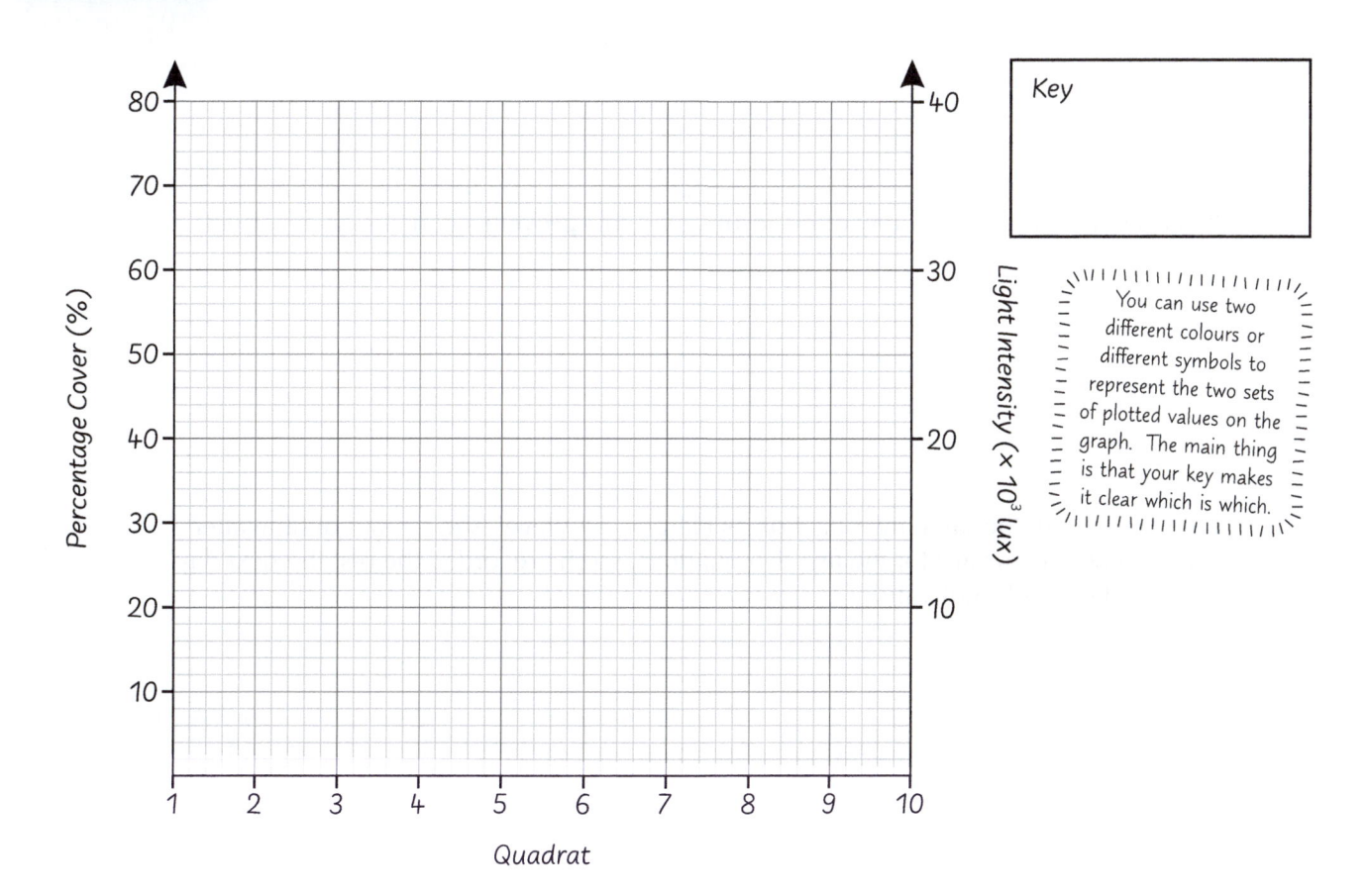

You can use two different colours or different symbols to represent the two sets of plotted values on the graph. The main thing is that your key makes it clear which is which.

© CGP — not to be photocopied

Practical 7: Field Investigations

Conclusions and Evaluation

Required Practical 7

Task 14 Harper concludes that a lower amount of light causes more moss to grow on the lawn. Think about whether his results **support** the hypothesis from Task 10.

Write one reason why they **do** support it.

....

....

Write one reason why they **don't**.

....

....

Task 15 **Evaluate** Harper's investigation by answering the following questions.

How could Harper improve the **validity** of his results, in order to better support his conclusion?

Key Definition
Valid results
Results that are repeatable, reproducible and answer the original question.

If Harper improves the validity of his results, will this **prove** his conclusion is correct?

Kate carried out the same investigation as Harper. However, she ran out of time after she recorded the results for the first five quadrats, so she recorded the rest the next day. Why are her results **not** valid?

Practical 7: Field Investigations © CGP — not to be photocopied

Conclusions and Evaluation

Required Practical 7

Task 16 Harper decides to repeat his investigation to see whether the percentage cover of moss on the lawn may also have been affected by **soil moisture** and **soil pH**.

Jot some notes below to suggest an **improved method** that Harper could use to determine whether the percentage cover of moss across his lawn may have also been affected by factors other than light intensity.

Hint: you can measure soil moisture using a moisture probe.

Task 17 Sana is investigating the **distribution** of some plants across a meadow using a **transect**. She records the plants that are touching the transect.
Her results for the section of transect shown below are in the table.

Section of transect

Key: Melancholy Thistle, Rough Hawkbit, Sweet Vernal Grass

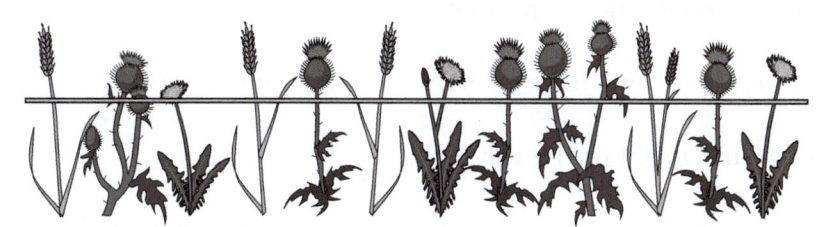

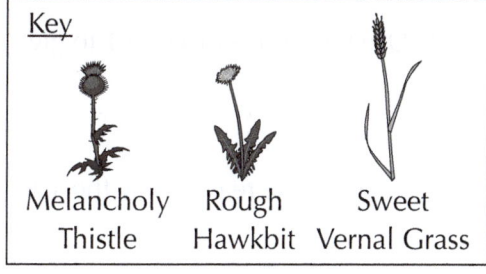

Organism	Number
Melancholy Thistle	7
Rough Hawkbit	4
Sweet Vernal Grass	5

What **error** has Sana made? How will it affect her results?

Think about what is being counted.

Watch out for angry plants — just leaf them alone…

DISCUSS The sampling techniques covered in this practical have limitations — with a partner, think of some situations where you couldn't use a quadrat or a transect to sample the number of organisms in a habitat. See if you can come up with some ideas for what you might be able to use instead in those situations.

© CGP — not to be photocopied

Practical 7: Field Investigations

Exam-Style Questions

Required Practical 7

Task 18 Try these **exam-style** questions.

1 Limpets are a type of marine snail that live on rocky shores.
A scientist investigated the population size of limpets in an exposed bay and a sheltered bay by marking out a 10 m by 10 m area in each bay and taking random samples using a quadrat.

The results of the investigation are shown in **Table 1**.

Table 1

Location	Number of limpets										Estimated population size
Exposed bay	5	6	17	10	11	1	4	8	6	15	?
Sheltered bay	40	52	29	45	33	26	50	39	22	46	7640

1.1 The quadrat used had an area of 0.5 m².
Estimate the size of the limpet population in the area sampled in the exposed bay.

.... limpets
[2]

1.2 State the dependent variable in this investigation.

....
[1]

1.3 Use the results in **Table 1** to give a conclusion for the scientist's investigation.

....
[1]

1.4 Suggest **one** reason why the scientist's results might not be valid.

....
[1]

1.5 Suggest **two** improvements the scientist could make to improve the validity of the results.

1. ....

2. ....
[2]

1.6 The scientist thinks that the distance from the shoreline is affecting the distribution of limpets in the sheltered bay. Suggest how the scientist could change the method to investigate this.

....

....
[2]

[Total 9 marks]

CGP books — they might just save your life...

OK, maybe not your *life*. But when it comes to exam revision, CGP are the undisputed champions. You can order any of our books and cards (with next-day delivery!) from us, online or by phone:

cgpbooks.co.uk • 0800 1712 712

Or you'll find our range in any good bookshop, including:

amazon.co.uk   WHSmith   Waterstones

0724 - 29509

CGP

Become a GCSE Biology Practicals pro — with CGP!

Give your practical skills a boost for AQA Combined Science Higher...

- **Tasks to boost your background knowledge...**
  So you can put your scientific thinking to the test

- **Activities on results, analysis and evaluation...**
  Yep — we've got every Required Practical covered

- **Exam-style questions for extra practice...**
  Of course — these will get you ready for the real thing!

- **Plus online sample answers for the whole book...**
  Perfect for seeing what you're aiming for!

Don't let your practical knowledge decay — CGP keeps a lid on it ☺

P.S. Don't miss our Required Practicals Course Booklets for GCSE AQA Chemistry and Physics!

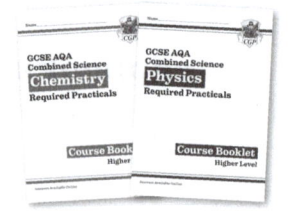

Roses are red, violets are violet

ISBN 978 1 83774 188 5

SCBAHPL41

www.cgpbooks.co.uk

Scan here for retail price